D0167238

Heaven and Earth

Heaven and Earth

A COSMOLOGY

Poems by

ALBERT GOLDBARTH

The University of Georgia Press

ATHENS AND LONDON

© 1991 by Albert Goldbarth
Published by the University of Georgia Press
Athens, Georgia 30602
All rights reserved
Designed by Betty Palmer McDaniel
Set in Aldus with Delphin display
The paper in this book meets the guidelines for
permanence and durability of the Committee on
Production Guidelines for Book Longevity of the
Council on Library Resources.

Printed in the United States of America

95   94   93   92   91   5   4   3   2   1

Library of Congress Cataloging in Publication Data
Goldbarth, Albert.
Heaven and earth : a cosmology : poems /
by Albert Goldbarth.
p.   cm.
ISBN 0-8203-1299-1 (alk. paper).—
ISBN 0-8203-1300-9 (pbk. : alk. paper)
I. Title.
PS3557.O354H4   1991
811'.54—dc20   90-45961
CIP
British Library Cataloging in Publication Data available

Acknowledgments

With thanks to the editors of the following journals, in which these poems (some in earlier versions) first appeared:

The American Poetry Review: "12th Century Chinese Painting with a Few Dozen Seal Imprints Across It"

The Beloit Poetry Journal: "The Nile"

Boulevard: "Desire Song," "Coin"

Caliban: "The History of Buttons"

The Carolina Quarterly: "Of Ontology"

The Cimarron Review: "A Florid Story," "How the World Works: An Essay"

The Denver Quarterly: "Why I Believe in Ghosts"

The Georgia Review: "Mishipasinghan, Lumchipamudana, etc.," "The Aliens' Translation Machine," " 'Too Much,' "

The Indiana Review: "The Alias: A Survey"

The Iowa Review: "An Explanation," "One Continuous Substance," "The Sciences Sing a Lullabye"

The Journal: "Forensics," "Los Verdados"

The Kenyon Review: "Burnt Offering," "Toil,"

The Michigan Quarterly Review: "Reality Organization"

New England Review/Bread Loaf Quarterly: "Pheletos of Cos"

Northwest Review: "Alien Tongue," "A Paean to the Concept"

The Ontario Review: "Spies (*Spies? Spies.*)," "The Niggling Mystery"

The Paris Review: "Domains"

Ploughshares: "Homage," "The Gate"

Poetry: "The Talk Show," "A Monument," "In the Midst of Intrusive Richness," "Steerage," "Sentimental," "Vigil," "A Letter"

Poetry East: "Little Burger Blues Song," "Some Things"

Poetry Northwest: "A Tale," "The Whole Earth Catalogue"

River City: "Another Portrait," "As Response"

The Southwest Review: "The Children of Elmer"

Vox: "The Dynamics of Huh"

The Yale Review: "Shawabty, Ushabi, or Shabti Figures"

Additionally, "The Whole Earth Catalogue" was awarded *Poetry Northwest*'s annual Theodore Roethke Prize; "As Response" received *River City*'s annual Hohenberg Award; "A Letter" and "The Alias: A Survey" were each reprinted in an annual edition of *The Pushcart Prize: Best of the Small Presses*; "The Nile" and "How the World Works: An Essay" were collected in *New American Poets of the Nineties* (Godine).

The publication of this book is supported by a grant
from the National Endowment for the Arts,
a federal agency.

Contents

Talk

Love

Talk

Why is "lenguage" "Ignatz"?
—Krazy Kat to Ignatz Mouse,
January 6 1918,
GEORGE HERRIMAN

The Talk Show

. . . in 1930, The Bell Telephone Company commissioned one of their employees, Karl Jansky, to find out why the new car radios suffered from static. Jansky set up radio antennae, and heard a steady hiss coming from the direction of the Milky Way. Radio astronomy was born thirty years later.

—JAMES BURKE

A woman "heard angels." The paper says angels
sussurra'd her body, rang their praises daylong
through its reedy places, stirred her
smallest water. And elsewhere, Larry
"Dude Man" Chavez raises his #2 wrench
indifferently overhead on the C-track tightening line,
and feels something like lightning—only
there isn't lightning—beam to the wrench head,
branch down his arm, make all of his muscles
electric feathers, then exit his other arm out
its guttering candelabrum fingers and into
the frame of the Ford. It's stored

there. It happens. We all know it happens.
The cops and the hospital nightshift crew know
what a full moon means, and
if their decades of statistics don't cut diddlysquat
with you, here's someone being wheeled in
from a 3-car smashup while the universe hums
its lunar kazoo, and adrenalin everywhere dervishes.
And statistics on sunspots, and suicides.
And statistics on lines of magnetic pull,
and conception. We're the few but beautiful
units of the first day of the cosmos
densed-up over time; when the lady I love

3

flaps suddenly in sleep like a wire discharging, it
makes sense as much as anything—bad dreams,
zinged nerves—to simply say *we're* where
the Big Bang ripples to the limits of a continuous medium,
flickers a little, kicks. I've disappointed her
sometimes; and so, myself. I've left the house then,
while she slept, and while my neighbors slept, as if
I could walk noise out of myself
through darkness, finally dialing-in
the talk show where the blood calls with its question,
and the "sky," whatever that is, whatever portion we are
of it or once were, answers. And

I've walked past where the university's planetarium
dish-ear swivels hugely for the far
starcrackle Karl Jansky more primitively
dowsed. It happens any size; that woman? picked up
cop calls on her IUD, the paper adds, in bubble-bursting
glee. Although if angels are voices beyond us
in us, everyone's umbles are singing hosannahs
under their everyday wamble and gab. I've
slipped back into bed some nights and clasped her
till I slept, then woke to her heart
in my ear, that mysterious sound,
on earth as it is in heaven.

Mishipasinghan, Lumchipamudana, etc.

Some days, anything is wonderful. In its
detail, in its conception, in its chainlink leading
into the rest of the physical and conceptual cosmos, anything
is wonderful. I'm reading
how the Quechua, in Peru, have a thousand words
for "potato." A thousand! For the new ones
with a skin still as thin as mosquito-wing, for
troll-face ones, for those sneaky burgundy corkscrews
like a devil's dick . . . And there can be
the opposite, yes. There can be a country
with a word like *peynisht*. It's said in a whisper.
Peynisht was the place political prisoners were sent,
a bleak wind-damaged plain, and by a history
of reference, *peynisht* has come to mean
the labor they perform there (for they're sent there yet),
a labor only found in the state-of-being called *peynisht*,
a daily toil without relief of any kind, or hope of pardon,
just this side of unbearable—*peynisht* is that
specific: the labor there, as exactly close to unbearable
as labor can be without crossing fatally over.
There's the sound of wind in the word, a wind with
salt inside that's whipped like spurs across people.
You might think it would be the perfect word
for loose appropriation—so a sour marriage,
a spat-embittered office job, a night of terrible
string-quartet performances in a room so small you
can't scratch . . . the way we use "hellish," these
would be *peynisht*. But it isn't so. It's only
that literal place and the literal spirit-deadening effort
going on there. A man's learned waking on time,
to avoid the clubs. He goes to the pile of stone,

and carries stone, and does nothing but carry stone
in a world without one friend or minute of respite,
and when it's dark he returns
to the dirt floor and its shit-hole and
they throw him a pan of bad water and a raw potato.
He eats it. And there's only one word.

A Tale

Syzygial is a good word; *defalcation,*
exfoliate, janizary—good words, all,
although I don't employ them. I never say
gunnysack, crepuscular, umwelt, rinkydink.
We think the light is plangent and say
wow. I think the light was very plangent
when I found her staring out the bedroom window
at the orange spine the sun makes
on the water as it sets. It set. She
kept on staring. What she saw wasn't important
then, I understood—what mattered
was simply the looking itself, whatever
of self-hypnosis and healing it held. I suppose
I was hurt, to be so excluded. There wasn't
a thing I could say. We'd failed at something,
we'd tried too much—I wanted to tell her this
was okay. There's a tale (I finally said)
about language. (Now she turned around.) Once
humans grunted; they flapped or jabbed
their hands. God saw this wasn't enough
for hosannahs, and let it be known
on a given day at a given minute, He would rain
down language on the Earth. The humans
showed up, each with a basket. Heaven
parted, and All of the Words That There Are
poured forth. No one received everything.
Mamihlapinatapei was gathered up
by Tierra del Fuegans. *Hozh'q* by the Navajo.
Whatever I've said in my life,
to you, or on paper, shrewish, grandiloquent,
small asshole-blats of expression, or

great breath-bearing indications of struggling thought,
the whole of it—these are the words
my people collected.
The cheap ones. The sweet ones. I like to believe
compassion slipped into their baskets.

The Dynamics of Huh

*The drummers of the Lokele who live in the jungle of
Zaire, not far from the former Congo River, still know
the sayings that fit their tom-tom rhythms. In fact they
need the sayings in order to drum the rhythms. But no
one now remembers what they mean—or whether they
ever "said" anything.*

—ILLICH AND SANDERS
in *ABC*

I can't begin to guess the contents of these U-Haul moving cartons
someone's dumped in a rush, abandoned in this gutter, but the pure
dumb blocky form of it is so eloquent of those few
yet truly hellish address-hopping years that followed the divorce
—assembling each new stinking retinue of cardboard flats
and wrapping, endlessly, wrapping until some first grayish dribble
of dawn, then wrapping more—that a column of heebie-jeebies,
like fire ants, rampages my spine. Or the 21st Indian

Intertribal Pow-Wow moaning soulfully out of the tv is
that box's incomprehensible substance—war?
peace? rain? it's obdurate Extraterrestrial to me—and even
so, this solemn ululating, in the way it ceremonially
assumes the human heart and godly ear connect, and
wrings a little blood, a little blood with wings, for the one
to be heard by the other . . . in this, it brings
completely back to me the old Jews on their New Year

in the willfully uncomfortable storefront Orthodox *shul*
my father favored when I was 10 or 11 and watching them
softly rock their prayer as if each slowdanced in place
with an angel, and listening as their opaque wall of Hebrew,
uttered brick by brick, rose out of the room to somewhere
I could never believe and they could never not. When I was

9

10, the common comicbook expression "Huh?"
might have stood for whole days of my life; once,

in that room where the apartment bulged enough
for the indulgence of an extra secondhand sofa—they called it
the sunroom—I came on my father weeping, my father
turning his wide face physically inside-out
by tears. I remember: the light, and the lace drapes, placed
a wavy veil over his eyes. And all he said
of it then or would ever say was just *One day
you'll understand,* words wobbly and much furzed-over. Well,
    one day

has come and gone, or maybe one day's really everyday eventually.
I've waked to see the woman beside me finely designed
along her upthrust haunch by sleepcreases
hieroglyphically alien, and evocative
of the whole encoded beings we are in the whole contextual
dazzling unbreakable code of social knottedness and night sky
we inherit. In a world like that, an insomniac man might
walk although it rains, although the Pow-Wow thousands

prayed all day for rain. He stops: the downpour's softened
the U-Haul boxes. As he looks, one fist of water sloshes through,
then opens, bearing a wickedly metal-studded leather corset,
a child's party hat with a paper spray of what seem cockatoo
rump-feathers, and a fraying plum-velvet New Testament he
nabs and finds inscribed with the names of 3 generations
in English, Finnish, and Arabic. Huh? It makes me
want to call my father, across the layers of shale,

worm-warren, and motherlode coal that separate us,
offering my much-thumbed Life/Death dictionary
so we can speak, and telling him simply how deeply I *know*
so much now, but I can't *understand.*

Alien Tongue

Proficient in writing the 20th century poem now, we
can say anything. *In my veins, ice*
is on fire. That's a good one. We can zero down
to the body saying its rosary the chromosomes
over and over. Ask us—anything. It's easy enough
lightdriving to the planet Alpha-Two. There,
amber bipeds not unlike us go about their business
under a binary sun. And there are two moons
also—"ovaries," one parlance has it. "Testicles,"
another. You can imagine the intricate shadows!
It's as if each person's the central pin
an hour-hand and minute-hand revolve from.
Not surprisingly, their language parses time
to an exquisite thinness—there's a tense
that means "I would have, if I'd been my twin."
Their houses are all a multichambered seedpod
about the size of one of our seaside bungalows
—each has been grown from a clan tree (it
would translate, roughly, "place-life-tree") and
these, as well as the special arboreal steroids
individual to a clan (and so producing dwellings
shaped to a clan's own temperament), are most
jealously guarded. Winter is bitter
(entire epic "drum-poem" cycles exist to implore
the spirits of thawing) but brief. The nearly
year-long summer is paradisal: flute-birds
hatch, the double sun runs thick as mayonnaise
in the boughs, and couples recognizing light tan
cross-clan natal stippling that the heat brings
to their thighs, pair off. They'd look like
any Earthlings in the bushes. Or, this

gray-haired grandma crouching on a pod-stoop,
weeping: surely she's no stranger to us.
I can see—she's hours past tears, by
now it's only the dry and shoulders-shivering
heaves that go on with a terrible, habitual
will of their own. What's wrong, I ask her. It's
simple. Her husband is dead, her "near-me-one" is
how it roughly translates. Only yesterday they
bound the hands that used to stroke her cheeks,
they bound them in funeral wire, and by that length
they lowered the corpse in its grave. Now
she's alone. And do you know what people are
like, she asks. When she was attending the burial rite,
when she was giving her life's last intimate touch
to that wire-tied figure, somebody, "beast-people,"
knowing the house would be vacated, entered it,
robbed her, left with a packet of clan pod seeds
and all of her meager savings. Then
she looks to me for reply. She's so small.
There's a stain in her eyes as if grief were a color.
These things happen on Alpha-Two.
I don't know what to tell her.

The Aliens' Translation Machine

Shayneh puhnim my grandmother said in her
evocative Yiddish, and she stroked that "pretty face"
she praised. *Chingate madre* a kid said
at the corner, and by intonation alone it
tore a hole in the air. *Toota-benna!* Vito of the pizzas
said, and truly did smack his fingertips,
then flick this kiss to the world. I was 6; I
couldn't believe they really didn't all *first*
think these things in English, and then
rapidfire convert it in their heads—as I'd do

combinations of tongue-taps on my palate
into multiplied numbers. Maybe the suspicion
I was wrong in this—whenever it occurred—that dawning
glimmer everyone wasn't a version of me
out there, but came from a place,
and went through a day, exquisitely alien . . .   maybe
that's the light that falls like a club through me,
finally, now, in a horrible fullness, and
these splinters of it ride the slow unwinding
of your tears. If I were you I'd stop

and reconsider, start to hum the unaddable sums
of the mantra of What's Still Strong and Lovely Between Us
while I (who'd be you) did too . . .   The error's
so sweet in those medieval-rendered Biblical scenes,
where time is crumpled up close, and Moses's robing,
or Judas's scattered examples of office decor, or
Esther's bedroom set, are those of the painter.
In an altarpiece done in the 1390s, Mary knits

a shirt for her child with needles 1,390 years early.
Maybe he'll cry then. Maybe she'll whisper in peasant French.

She strokes his wetted cheek . . .   The painter has given them
both such pretty faces.

The Nile

Elijah this.
The Children of Israel that.
And Moses. Moses in the bulrushes, Moses
blahblahblah. The doors closed
and the dark, fake-woodgrain paneling casketed us
away from the world for an hour and 45 minutes every afternoon
in Rabbi Lehrfield's neighborhood Hebrew School. Here, as one,
the pious and the derelict chafed equally. The vehicle
of Rabbi Lehrfield's narrative drive was Obedience,
all the wonder in those stories was run down methodically
and left behind like so many roadkills. Methuselah
something. Somethingsomething Ezekiel. And Pharaoh
set the infant Moses in front of a crown and a plate of embers,
testing if this was the child it was prophesied
would steal his reign. And Moses
did reach for the crown. But the Lord set an angel to guard him,
who now did guide that hand to lift an ember, and so did Moses
thereby burn his tongue and lo would stammer all his life long.
Did I care? *His speech limped, but he lived.*
Did I listen? Every night I'd read another chapter
in those actionful schlock-epic books by Edgar Rice Burroughs,
the ones where Mars (Barsoom, the natives call it) is
adventured across by stalwart Terran John Carter, *Jeddak*
(Warrior-King) and husband of the gauzy-saronged and
dusk-eyed Dejah Thoris, Princess of all those red-duned climes.
It made more sense to me
than God is a great bush of fire. All the while
Moses stuttered in front of the Living Flame, I
silently practiced Martian. It was Rabbi Lehrfield's
Martian School for me the whole lackluster time.

Out of what we've learned to call
"deep structures," Lindsay Nichol, my niece, is pursing
the first of her organized sounds. They're . . . oh,
no words; but they take sure place in a pattern
as repeated as the crib bars, with a little
occasional lingual fillip
as decorative as the headboard's gnomish carving.
Slurp and gurgle, out of whatever
increasingly subatomic deliveryline of chevals
flashes the message of neural language-wiring on up
from meiotic gel unbroken to this 9-month-old
soliloquizer, Lindsay Nichol
is wailing, gooing, composing juicy musics, here
on the quantifiable, witnessed edge of a process that
starts somewhere magic. —Someone
pointing to a tree, and saying: "tree," a heart, and: "heart,"
the first time; being with a word so new it's glass
not fully hardened yet, it's going to be a tree soon, or a heart,
but now it's rainwater, and the morning sun is living yolk in
        its skin . . .
                    In Moccasin County,
once, the night a full moon orb'ed the giant crosshairs
of a steeple, and any spirit-commingling was possible, and the line
between the Trinity and 3 tossed shots of cornmash likker
wavered in tremulous hoochiecoo veils of feeling . . . I could see
such language settle out of the air. They spoke in tongues. A woman
frenzied like a telegraph key on the sawdust-clumped church floor.
Galvanic bluebolts straight from Heaven twitched her limbs.
A man was shaking like sheeted foil. What they said was
clearly speech, although I didn't know the words
/M'lash k'HAB chebawby HEI-HEI-HEI ZH'BO/ was clearly
not a sloshy gibberish, but something
from the templates in the brain that give us English, only
singular and more shimmering with its source: a kind of
manna spangled over their tongues. If anything

I've also seen comes close, it's in films of some early
jazz guys jamming through the thirties, with the drapes
of cigarette smoke in those backroom clubs befuddling the stage,
and joy and concentration being the same thing, and
between their rumpled and utterly brotherly selves
a field I can only call "vocabulary" occurs and unites
and they play, in great asyncopated waves,
where the cells of the blood are notation,
where the nerves of the body are staves . . .
                                        I have this
daydream: squares and circles and triangles
floating out of the sky. My friends
are lifting them. Licking them. Taking intimate
oral pleasure off of these perfect lines. And after that,
nothing is ever the same. We're marked.
We've nursed on the "high structures" Plato says
precede the smutched units of Earth.

———————

In my family, stories are normally softened
over the years. —As if a tragedy,
or even adrenalin-jetting celebration, any
abandoning of the blandest mean, was shameful.
By the time my life is second-hand
or third- explained to Lindsay, I'll be
anyone, and flatter than the nondescript stone marker.
Once I met my cousins Izzy and Rebecca,
only once—they'd come in for a wedding.
They were in their middle-70s then, 2 crease-faced German Jews
from when a Jew in Germany meant you wore a number
dyed into your arm. And so I heard some stories directly.
"They were after me," he says. "I wasn't afraid
from their fists. But some had broken bottles. See."
He lifts his shirt. "I hid in a barrel. A barrel

of pigshit. Yes, really. It covered my head. In this, even
they didn't search. The worst part was the burning
against the cut, this pigfire, filthfire, eating my skin.
But then they gave up and I crawled out. It's a blur then,
really, until Becka and America." She says, "My mother
begged my sisters not to get into the truck. One was 15.
Meeseleh, she was only 12. The driver told her, 'You
think you'll miss them so much, you get in too.' She
did, without a second's hesitation. In part, I think, to get them
all on their way before I was discovered in the haypile.
Well of course—they went up the chimneys, in the Camps.
Who knows what went on in those places? 20 years later,
we were in New Jersey then and settled, a neighbor
gave me a little set of scented soaps, and I saw on the box
they were made in Germany, and—Izzy will tell you
it's true—I threw up. For a week after that, I threw up."
To reach America, they "did things" too—"not so nice,
if you want to know. These were not pretty times."
There are anecdotes of innocent German countryside couples
clubbed for their clothes. The irony is, they
reached their haven, Liberty lifting her torch high,
just when anti-German sentiment reached its peak.
"And so our accents—you know? For years
Americans beat us up in the streets." He shakes his head
as if the past could be shooed like a fly.
"So, anyway. Everyone's here for the wedding, a happy time,
now let's be happy." He hooks his arm around Rebecca's arm.
His speech limped, but he lived.

God doesn't speak in the language of people
or need to. God speaks out of what first hurt us.
So of course, on the mountain, Moses understood
what was said by the fire.

I'm 40. I know, by now, my life, my friends' lives . . .
we will never wake to face some all-consuming
deific announcement. But I also know: hurt is inevitable.
Then: so is some Godtalk, sized to that hurt.

Now Lindsay's asleep, and quiet, quiet . . .
Finally the long dark river of night
will deliver her crib to its tanglement
in the first pale reeds of the morning.

"The more you're meat, the less they treat you human," Kendall says
amid the general beer-tone party brouhaha. She's
just been hired as a hospital's Emergency Unit desk clerk.
"If you come in with a broken leg they'll talk to you
while setting it, explain things, chat. But
someone comes in mangled from a tractor toppling over and he's
just bloodied-up parts to assemble." This is all
new to her. She ledges out her lower lip in concentration.
"I suppose there are reasons." Later,
                              an hour maybe, I
see her hazily through a window. She's left the gaudy talk and
rock-&-roll, and walks by herself in the midnight yard,
around the substantial base of its guardian tree.
She's talking softly—to herself—or to some self-of-her
that's taken form invisibly out of the molecules of the night, and
walks beside her. Kendall's
musing. She's "working things out." Whatever
infinite hallways of pain and laboring tissue she's seen opened
in the bodies wheeled past her for the last week, these
are first inventing words to hold
small conversation with her. Moonlight's
whittled by the bough to a handspan conical shape; and
Kendall halts as if to press her ear against this

hearing-trumpet floating in the blackness, and be privy
for a moment to the murmurstuffs the electrons of Earth
exchange with the protons of Luna.

Soon
she's back: she's wagging ass to some sperm-powered shout
in an early Rolling Stones hit. What I come
to understand, though, is that everyone—these
friends o' mine, my tender lads and lassies—needs some time
outside, alone, by the tree, in its Whispering Zone.
Now Casey leaves the very public hubbub for this quiet
domain, now Rita . . .   Some of them touching the bark
that's textured like the rope sole of an espadrille,
and some of them simply moving their lips in silence,
under stars that must be Cosmic Esperanto's
punctuation. "Albert, YO!"—I'm

back in Stonesville,
avocado chip dip, argument, flirtation. When I look
next time, a 14-year-old boy is in the yard. He's . . .
a translucent 14-year-old boy. So shy.
So pained by anything in this world. No wonder
he's practicing Martian. "Thark," I hear him say
in a familiar cracking voice. "Tars Tarkas. Jasoom."
No wonder I love these friends I have now. When
I start to say a word of encouragement to him, he
distorts into a mist, he's air now, and my single gasp
inhales him . . .

No wonder I love my people. We're
all woozy-eyed with partying by now, we're tired
empathetic heaps lounged out on the pillows . . .
My sweeties, my grownups who have come so far, what are we
here in midlife, but
the scars of healing from where we once burned

our tongues on the Other Language.

Love

The primeval being was round and had four hands and four feet, back and sides forming a circle, one head with two faces, looking opposite ways, set on a round neck and precisely alike; also four ears, two privy members, and the remainder to correspond. This was the man-woman. But Zeus, in punishment for attacking the gods, cut the being in two, as you might divide an egg with a hair. Now each of us when separated is always looking for his other half. And when one finds the other half, the pair are lost in the desire for intercourse, and for something else which the soul desires and can not tell, and of which she has only a dark and doubtful presentiment. And the reason is that human nature was originally one and we were a whole and the desire and pursuit of the whole is called love.

—PLATO,
reworked from the
Benjamin Jewett version

But there was a time, in the very early universe, when the temperature was above a few hundred times the mass of the proton, when the symmetry hadn't yet been broken, and the weak and electromagnetic forces were all not only mathematically the same, but *actually* the same. A physicist living then, which is hard to imagine, would have seen no real distinction . . .

—STEVEN WEINBERG
on cosmology symmetry theory,
in an interview

Desire Song

The graspy heart, that lobster of ours that
wants, and wants, and is evolved to lust
for one grain shat by a swallow in flight
as much as the whole packed 4-story silo.
There's a cloud across the moon tonight
like the skin boiled milk gets
cooling—slightly blue and slightly wrinkled.
I want the glass of warm milk from my childhood
carried up to the crib by a living Grandma Nettie
with her hair still singed in odor
from the frightening tines of her old-fashioned curler,
yes, and I want the moon
in its entirety, the moon through the windshield
detailing Phyllis's breast for me the first time
it was more than a wish or a centerfold
peeked in private, yes, I want the moth of faint veins
holding her nipple, the corruscations it made
in stiffening, casting complicated shadows within itself
not unlike the moon, which I want,
and that '63 Chevy we parked in, which I want,
and the father who loaned it to me that night,
who I want waiting up for me, walking the planet
instead of being one more battery slipped inside it,
powering the rest of us, who are sweating our sheets
with our wanting. Michael tells me:
in the slammer—call it what you like, the pen,
the hoosegow, the big house, call it shit city—
you want *anything* from outside, and
a used-up tube of lipstick or the one-eyed spaniel's water pan

can hold the same desire a limousine does.
He's seen kneeling men lick cell bars
for the salt a visitor's palm left.
Think of the ribcage . . .   think of the lobster
clacking inside its trap.

Of Ontology

The bruises are beautiful really: orchid, plum, bordeaux.
We need them. These are the overlush flowers of blood we bid
float broken through our pale skins when talk of divorce gets
physical and drunk. And we need that talk—that pain
in the range of our comprehension. There are other flowers,
lichen smears, that live off rock and height, at the unthinkable
line where planet ends and God's ordered heavens begins,
if there's a God and if there's order in that frightening foulard
of dark and crucible-fires up there . . .   no wonder

we choose familiar hurt. At times I've known it sure
as anyone: that August at the beach, when we were
reaching the final weeklong-held cacophony-note in a year
of absolutely wounding squabble . . .   at the edges where
our love-stuffed suffering stopped, there was a silence
so articulate in describing ideas of entropy,
malignant tumors milktooth-sized, oblivion and chance,
we'd hear it in between two waves and redouble
our pots-and-pans duet of damaging clamor. And

M. and C., who lug their dead marriage to parties, the
better to raise its rich, pit-retch dissection-stink in public.
And H., her fist all night at her father's fat door, come
out you sonofabitch come out, all night until
the cops squealed up in that earliest, watery dawn
when the sky is like fluid leaked from a clubbed fish.
And W., quit his 6-figure job, bummed freights,
settled down with his ex, left, took a male lover,
left, returned to his bigtime exec desk, quit . . .   Each,

a bruise. And some are canned-peas-green with
swine's-eye-pink mottled into the center. And some
are mulberry-blue with carnelian shot through. And one is a
perfect coal-and-indigo feather fit in skin
the unspeakably delicate ivory color of first tusk . . .
Each, a sweet diversionary trauma. Kings
don't war for beds of gold-and-pearl, a king once said:
they war to keep their beds from floating into the soul-eating
emptiness between stars. One night I woke

inside an August after-midnight where the waters ditto
those sparks in the sky so truly, there's no up or down and living is
being lost in space. I slipped our wicker bed and walked the sands
where we were also roughly repeated: some young couple,
"you did," "I didn't," "you sure the fuck did"—they hugged
that bicker to their chests like blankets fighting cold.
Eventually, I even heard some slaps. And so they had them
then—a small bouquet of bloodflowers
rooting them, naked and obdurate, into the here-and-now. And

of course the opposite happens. The sun was naked burning.
At noon, some guy sprawled flat on a dune
and started talking to the air. To the column of air
he was the base for, talking all the way to whatever conceptual
cornicework of the universe he held up. I could see,
it was easy, he'd been hurt in love—sexual or parental or
who-knows-what-or-why, but hurt. From too much of this world.
He was spreadeagled, open, he deliquesced like a tablet
so happily into the wide, light fields of ontology.

A Monument

It's a weak chargray-and-camellia dusk
when we start lugging out the corpses.
How at a party you'll fly off into your 4th white wine
and be lost for the evening. When I still went
down to Mexico with Tony though they needed to run more
tests on your chest. Who spends most blindly.
All of the corpses, starting with the old ones that are really
only fossils now, the chalk and lime
suggestions of a grievance. Even the smallest ones, that died
straight after their first inhalation and scream—the size
of yams in our hands, and we're bringing them one
by one to the living room, propping them up,
filling the air with their foxfire. Now the sky is
doing the same: is hefting, faithfully, its store of bodies
up for staged display. Against the black, that
archer, virgin, regent, take on size their damaged lives had only
dimly hoped for—now they burn
along their skins at definitive
ganglion-knots or open wounds or love-pinches
in a resplendence, their original
resuscitators having borne them overhead with grander
honorific and expiatory design than
we, inside our charnel-house, can manage.
Callisto, Cassiopeia, Orion: limb by limb,
re-membered. Under stars like these,
while the sensible burghers of Paris snored and the world was
given over to the twiddle of roach and mantis, Gericault
dragged his sacked cadavers
from the hospital morgue to pose inside
his studio—knew their arms, draped, weighty, stone
bolognas chilling his nape—and fussed

their wretched flesh until it met his compositional
desires. Some stank. A few were entering blue. All
turned, beneath his flinchless vision, to the 15
passengers left of 149 the crew had sentenced
peremptorily to a raft and then abandoned. Now that raft,
exact in mockup, fills his floor. And now
his sad bespraddled lovelies fill the raft—he's had
a witness list positions, all 15, the dead, the living,
interstacked. And giving everything to this;
he's shaved his head in devotion. He lotions one
hard arm: he's learned this picks his lamplight's accents
out in a semblance of life. And now he opens that hand
—like a beast on its back, attempting a miniature
last dignity. Did they talk about home?
Did they care where they shat? All night, with them,
with the waters off Senegal rising to pull at his knees
until the sun shows and the stars blank past their vanishing point,
and still he's huffing under more bundles,
shuffling, finicking, corpse on corpse, a monument to work
toward and away from.

Little Burger Blues Song

In my own, familiar kitchen, at a quarter to midnight,
one night, where the spearpoint pilot light rises staunch
as a hood ornament, and the day-old meatloaf sandwich gives
the countertop the air of an autopsy slab,
and the cockroach zigzags, and the faucet stammers,
and from his 1950s diner sign
the chubby bun-cheeked face of Mr. Cheeseburger sings
in red delight "Am I Good!" . . . the phone. The phone
erases all normality in ringing, and before I even hear
the sweetly boozey blame in Morgan's voice, the lines
defining these objects I know grow slightly faint,
as if smudged by a swipe of artgum. Morgan
wants to remind me, I said I would loan her a hundred. Yes,
but that was when we were married: I didn't
ask her to drag our seamsplit love to a lawyer. But
a promise is a promise, isn't it? Yes, of course, but
the people who made that promise are dead—the sour
carbonation of a bad longdistance Southwest Bell connection
is the limbo they've been sentenced to. I see her
curled to no more than a lima bean beneath the ratty afghan.
But you got my car. But it wasn't *really* "your" car.
But it was *my* father's money. Finally I don't know which
side I'm arguing. Neither does Morgan. Talk clicks
off. It's tomorrow by ten dark minutes. I'm alone
with a couple of dimwit stars and the brown-vested coroner who
presided over the meatloaf's carcass, Dr. Jack Daniels.
I can see now I was wrong: my friend Mr. Cheeseburger doesn't
have an exclamation point like a Fred Astaire dancing cane
lifted beside him—no. He's asking me one of the ancientmost

questions, and maybe the hardest of them.
Am I good? With each sip he answers less sure. The night
will eventually call it a day, and the cockroach doze happily
inside its shell, but my self-assessing friend,
if he's done at all, if he's ever done, won't be done well.

An Explanation

They say this really happened, in the Church of Eternal Light:
a penitent dropped to the floor wearing nothing but sweat, she
spasmed like some snake on an electrified wire, she uttered
angel eldestspeech, and then she disappeared—they mean
totally, and at once. First the entire tarpaper room gave a shudder,
and then she disappeared—at once, and totally.
Nobody understands it. Well,
maybe I understand it. Once, in 8th grade, Denton Nashbell
had an epileptic seizure. Mrs. Modderhock squatted
above where he flapped like something half a person
half a pennant, she was pressing a filthy spoon to his tongue.
I've remembered him 25 years now. And—that woman? she
was the universe's tongue the universe
swallowed. That's as good an explanation as any.
Once, in sleep, you started a dream soliloquy,
the grammar of which is snow on fire, the words are
neuron-scrawl, are words the elements sing to their molecules . . .
—I threw myself across you.
It wasn't sex this time. I just wanted to keep you
beside me, in this world.

In the Midst of Intrusive Richness

"Buzzing the language of batteries, a batteryesque
blue-black, this mud-dauber wasp in the corner" a 1950s
poem might typically, topically start. That insect
is going to be amazingly likened to any number of gizmos
heretofore unassociated with wasphood—then a breathy
waft of philosophy is going to tumble it out of sight and
back, a decorationpiece attached to the slamming
shut of closure. I like it. Every poet goes a waxy bit

nostalgic. Wordsworth, thumping through the hill brush
with his alpenstock (and Coleridge), in soliloquizing
pursuit of a poetry new to the times, a speech the real,
gingivitised mouths of men might really utter, turns
in his writing continually from manufactory London,
ginswill alleys with their pussytalk patois, and
yearns in his elegant way for the days of Roman
shepherds supplicating Roman gods. So

every complicated Now is simple—once it's Past.
I only want to say the naked curvilinear
plenitude of Skyler under the sheets is a mighty
fine thing this afternoon, the call of tit to tongue is
mutual undeniably, sun in rungs
through the venetians reassembles on the bed,
and in the corner a wasp hums up the small mud
yurt he's architecting; all, so simple. But the too-much

world is with us. We know: electronmicroscopic
mites like rhinoceri breed in our eyelashes; there are tides
on Io 300 feet high—of *solid rock,* as Jupiter
scoots by, tugging; both times when police consulted

the Wonder Horse it was able to tap its especially-contrapted
typewriter board, predicting where the corpses of missing
children would be found (they were); the spatulate
footprints of yeti have been video'd; and human bodies

melted in the Allied bombing of Hamburg, *melted*,
ran along the melted asphalt, floating their own bones.
We know it all, and if we don't we can retrieve it
from media storage. There are days I grieve for everyone
in the midst of intrusive richness. All the horrible glory
of Godhead sometimes gets toyed to the size of a dashboard
figurine or necklace pendant and I know why. I
think I think of Wordsworth that way, yes or

Keats: in a little diorama-box I keep in my head,
he's writing. London's summer light is made a firm oar-handle
through the shutters, and its paddle-end is dazzlingly lifting
words to the white page surface. All goes well, or
poorly nobly. The poet opens his window and searches
London streetmurk for the right word. At the nearer eaves
a mud-dauber oscillates such blackberry sheen, it seems to be
an ink comprises it, *this* ink. It dips and rises.

Forensics

It looks like the mulberry's shadow. In fact it's the mulberry's
droppage, some still plump and entire, some half-decomposed
to ink. It's 5:55 in the awful bleared primordial
a.m. of the day. The sun first cranking up its pitch.
Some birds just starting to gargle rehearsal notes.
And the plant doors you'll be walking out of into
my red-webbed eyes in 5 more minutes. I'm
scared. I know, I *know*, it's nothing but rigamarole

car troubles calling me here to chauffeur you
home and we'll both slide lid-eyed down the chute
the bed is, into sleep—car troubles and troubleless love
have placed me in this little vigil, no big deal,
I know. But there was once another mix not much
unlike this early light still glossing off objects,
this impatient waiting for somebody, what the details
are doesn't matter; it happened repeatedly: she

would lean her forehead on the car's glass as if
hoping it was blank enough and cool enough this time
to leach her thoughts away completely, I
would sit behind the wheel saying crazy things, arraigning
things, to the sky; and then such tears and weary
deployment of facial defenses as you can imagine.
That's the way it happens, I'm sorry: be 5 and damping
your pants as the fire department matter-of-factly

nabs you from a topmost branch, and 35 years later
when the ferris wheel brings you by calliope-tapetracked
graduated stages to that same height, you will really
turn to your lover who's oohing in pleasure and really

vomit two hotdogs, a cola and green cotton candy into her lap:
a friend as brimmed with strength as anyone I know once told
        me this
when scotch outbalanced shame. I understood, I think
we all do. The forensics crew lifts fingerprints

from skin these days, a coup of '80s chemistry
the classic hardboiled "gumshoes" "shamuses" "dicks"
of the '30s and '40s, getting blackjacked into coocooland
on the trail of boots through mud, would have
dismissed as dreamy pie-in-the-sky, yet
understood about as well as anyone: we wake
some nights in the grip of invisible thumb-sized
eddies closing on our throats . . .   the sworls
that print us from fraught intimacy

years back. It's why we need to smile against
the tiredness, lean into each other inside the car
for a moment as if Brancusi's "The Kiss" were an i.v. bottle
feeding our bodies, be tender, love what's
now. I say this because at least 8 miles and that many
hours away, while we're asleep, some man
will see the shit dripped on his oak-lined street is chalky
mulberry color, stain carries so far.

Burnt Offering

*Rembrandt's friend, the physician Tulp, writes of "a
distinguished painter (who) was under the delusion
that all the bones of his body had softened to such a
flexibility that they might easily buckle like wax"—
his report dates this case of "melancholia" to the same
months' gap for which we have no record of any
Rembrandt work.*

This is how we fought:
we clambered into his oil *The Slaughtered Ox*,
we had knives, no not exactly
knives but we loved each other and so knew enough
to cut deep. The ox was flayed, beheaded,
pole-strung to the four quarters. In it,
we went for each other, there were no rules:
the weapon we had was intimacy.
With the gore of it smeared on our faces.
With its red meat pustules jeweling our lips.
We climbed the monumental sternum tiers,
we reached the pit of it, the nave,
the lightless center the rectal-hole
and the fluttery phlegm-edged esophagus-hole
both bleed toward. Nothing stopped us.
First we skinned each other. Slowly,
in spirals, deliberately as a peach.
A meat peach. A blood peach. The fruit of an ox.
With its ribs like a Viking ship's.
With its mucoused trusses and bellpulls.
In that air where each cell's ghost stinks.
First we skinned each other and
then we shucked whole muscles off.
It hurt, it was good. We used our teeth,

36

it was tasty. We pulled long fibers out
and their tissuey skreeking was music.
In the hall of its chandelier seminal vents.
In its buttery ducts. In its chancel.
First we skinned each other and
then we shucked whole muscles off.
In its rendering troughs. With ox fat under our nails.
And then we went for the bones.

He
was melting. Inside. His bones were turning wax. He grabbed the
worm-holed, nap-worn cap and the wharfmaster's cape he favored,
and left to walk the city, to let its hard sights harden him. The wind
today was brisk. Late fall. A goosepimple blue snuffled up the good
burghers' legs and under their good wives' skirts. He watched a gang
of teamsters push an overburdened sledge up one of the city's steepest
bridges—he wanted to sketch their curses blossoming into the cool air
like peonies, wanted to charcoal away at the gait of the one throwing
grease-soaked rags beneath the sledge's runners to lube its ascent. He'd
done the bridge before, the imperturbable look of its stone. All the
bridges of Amsterdam were stone. All public buildings and churches
and most of the finer houses were brick or stone. Yet the city was
built on a swamp. He knew that it could give in, any day, to that
essential softness. He could give in. He was melting, inside. If one
of the little shitty urchins chunked a stone at his back, he'd pour out,
he'd tip like a mold at the chandler's. This wouldn't do. He turned
back toward the Jewish quarter, off St. Anthoniesbreestraat—he knew
some of these people. He'd feel at home. A home is hard, his home
is filled with true hard things, it has shape. A hall of plaster casts of
goddesses; the waist-high garden statue of a child peeing; his chest
of petrifactions and animal skulls; his gold helmets, the halberds and
pikes, the various crowns and chalices, his Japanese armor; his mobile
of the universe done in chalk spheres circling a lustrous cherrywood

core. This house—the family was friends of his. He looked through the window. A small self-portrait he'd given them was framed on a wall. He looked at himself. He was scared. It was Friday. Their Sabbath was starting. The woman in the window bent her lace-shawled head in prayer and lit the pair of ritual candles. The wax. He was blinded. They found him curled like a dog on the cobbles, chilled but otherwise robust, although he claimed his knees could not support him, so wouldn't they carry him, please, inside, and then he'd walk home, when the Sabbath candles were melted and he rehardened, then he knew he could walk home.

And slept.
And dreamed we were back
at Barbara and David's. In my dream,
as in our "real time" with them in July,
the lights went out. Three square blocks of St. Louis,
kaput. So all night, then,
by one wan scrounged-up candle
at the center of us, and booze-glow: talking,
what do you think of, talking, but you're wrong,
do you see, no it's women who do that, talking,
once I did, of course you see, until the border
of any one of us didn't stop at the skin and whatever
othercreaturely compound-mind we made, it
floated the porch itself beyond
the borders of being a porch, on the long black hours.
There was a moment—everything
was possible. I looked: or you looked: our bodies were filled
by burning candles, we sat talking around
a single communal bone.

I wake, I see
sleep's paired us, leg
in leg—we're like a giant synesthesia,
making little sense together but making it,
making it anyway. By this I understand
the grief is burnt away again, we can be easy, truly
empty of it and easy, a while.
You murmur . . . something—not kissably yet, you murmur
like a tailor from a mouth that's gripping pins, but
meant sweet. Now we have to trust
such meaning. In the room where I keep
art book repros, photos and postcards tacked, the thin
flat light of daybreak first starts recognizing its own deeper
self in his portraits.
                            This young ghetto Jew
stares out at the world in such a delicately poignant
trick of chiaroscuro, we can see that really he
looks in: to where his bones, the stacked moth
spinal column bones, and the colonnade bones of the legs,
and the hummingbird skeleton whole in the middle ear,
and the rest, are part of the mysterious shipment
everyone delivers, at last, to that great reliquary
the planet . . .
and then past his bones: to where
our daily dole of endurance,
complicity, clouded-over good intentions, and ability to hurt
and be hurt are cupped from their bottomless well,
these, yes, and something else, the kind of dazzling sadness
when a spring breeze whuffs the cemetery dust
across a girl's dripsugar pastry
fresh from the bakery, so both
are on the lips her beau licks greedily in the sunlight . . .
This is also in the face of Thomas Jacobsz Haaring,
bailiff at the Amsterdam Court of Insolvency; and

in the face of Burgomaster Jan Six; and
in the finely grained, contained face of Margaretha de Geer.
How open,
   how soft,
must anyone be to see this and
record its velvety, mottled illumination? Or
maybe I mean how hard,
to stand the task? Or don't we live
where the two are one, and the fury of needing to hold them
simultaneously shakes us with such breakage,
we're ever crying to offer up
one or the other unto the gods, a flame, a waft,
we think will leave us
feeling some one thing purely . . .
       A postcard
showing The Rapture is pinned to the corkboard.
Possibly you've seen it: helterskelter cars
with corpses at their wheels, and something
albumeny-white, as slinky as skinks,
steaming out of those marvelous bodies.

———————

Now you wake. Now you work. Now you lay yourself down.
Another day gone up like smoke.

A Paean to the Concept

On show tonight, the maestrochef in his puffpastry headgear
veers a flapjack cunningly through a high arc like a porpoise-breach,
from right pan into left then back, the flapjack taking on
the sinuous wiffle a unicellular creature swims with, finally
taking on unbroken rushing grace of a pour
of water itself; the chef by now is one with it, is boneless
background motion, giving just the tilt and rhythm
of one of those rubber-ball-attached-by-a-rubber-string-to-a-paddle
champions, in whom we see the current and its banks are of
a piece. Across the restaurant, a not dissimilar power

to enchant is on display: this jive conniver guy
can't pay for a buttery shortstack happily downed, and
the narrative how and why of his wallet's coming up
zilch nobody quite believes (though everybody brings
a very willing fascination to his weasling, half-arrived
at the decision it's adequate payment). "Weasling" is right;
his story slinks through chinks in logic with a sneaky
and predacious—but essentially lovely and mink-like—
ductility. Free at last (the meal and its full consumer,
both) he thumbs a fitfully chugging ride to the People's Free

Clinic; it's the end shift, and his doctor palps
his pelvic meat and pipettes his serum with
routine in her face belying the absolutely dancerly
pas de deux of her hands. Shift done, she taxis home,
completely trusting in the zags the cabbie deftly zigs through town.
It's dawn; the first fogged edge of dawn. A jay
rebukes her as she walks the lawn. And there's Fat Tabby
(Fat Pussy, *he* says—nasty man) to be a momentary

fur stole at her ankles. Up the stairs now, into bed
beside that "nasty man" she loves, who I've adroitly

placed here dozing after his own tough night
of flapjack-juggling for slackjawed yokel diners.
They'll sleep, they'll wake, and we'll avert our eyes
thereafter, while their bodies slip together
into something so supple and accurate, there
isn't any word, although I see now how this whole poem
is a paean to the concept, and a word I've used already
has to do. By now, the cabbie zooms some new fare,
wheeling, weaving, assured—adroit. A
funny word. The cat goes for the bird. Adroit.

Another Portrait

What if Lowell's poem "My Last Afternoon with Uncle Devereux Winslow" were instead entitled "My Last Afternoon with Uncle Morris Shapiro," or his "Terminal Days at Beverly Farms" were instead entitled "Terminal Days at Grossinger's"?

—JOSEPH EPSTEIN

"The *kugel* was good" ("Good, good, good, always with
the 'good' " my Aunt Dinah is thinking, "and now
he's going to give with his famous line like Moses
reporting straight from Upstairs") "but the *knishes*,"
and this he drags out, the *kniiiiishes*, voice
on the wing and eyes agleam so you know he's leading
with hyperactive thespianship toward accolade,
"the *knishes* were" his hand lifts
with the stately pace of a levitated magician's assistant
(handshimmy gesture) "nyaah, so-so."
                                                 That's
my Uncle Morris Shapiro. The family is nothing
but an intricate device for transmitting
stories about him. Usually they're at some beachside resort,
everybody is saturated with statuary portions
of the chopped liver there, some unctious comic ("always
with the sex" my Aunt Dinah is thinking) is long offstage,
and at the hour when even an ad exec or a bail bondsman
wonders if there's God and why good people suffer etc.,
Morris Shapiro walks alone along where the ocean nonstop
fans its cards out on the table. Uncle Morris, alone with the night.
I know. I saw him. From a low hill I watched Morris Shapiro
face the full moon with his own full face, as if
a client ("I don't care if my client's the Pope or
whoever, he's gotta play honest by me") needs

being stared down, because of some indiscretion.
Uncle Morris Shapiro, that bathrobed protagonist, asking
the darkness—on all our behalves—The Tough Questions: Where
do our parents "really" go when we lower their boxes
into the earth? How
ennobling is shame, or is it? Why,
and out of what, are we sweetswindled into having such
a colloquy as this with the Invisible Forces About Us?
—and so on and so forth. I began walking toward him, there
where the moon was playing him like a lure
for all of the planet's insomniac malcontents and philosophers.
He was rocking a little, as if at the weary but intimate
end of a marathon dance, his arms around his partner
Miss Night Air, his eyes it seemed around some newfound
understanding, and just as I reached him (all that time
in the belief my approach was unsuspected) he spun, he
clutched my arm, and in a wildness, said "Boychick,
I've seen it! Buy Amalgam Electrical, then sell
in two weeks. Just *truuuuust* me." *That's* my Uncle
Morris Shapiro. Or

                    was it the other way around? So much
is lost across those thirty years of ocean fog and the kitchiekoo
wiggle of steam columns over the chicken broth. Sometimes
the story goes like this: I find him in the Game Room
after his late-night plate of blueberry *blintzes*, Morris
holding court with the rest of the poker regulars,
Sol, Nate, Herman and one guy they called Ballbuster Reno,
no one knew why. The fate of the civilized world rides
on these dollar bets; at that, though, they're just thin
excuse for the talking ("Talk, talk, talk" my Aunt Dinah is
thinking in her sleep somewhere nearby, and turns
to let the seabreeze brushing through the curtains
baste her other side). The talk is the usual Poker Talk, it's
taxes, and ungrateful children, and cutrate upholstery fabric,
and taxes, and two ripe melons hooboy on that redhead waitress

working by the Banquet Hall she has enough for an army (wink), and
taxes, and what's with this crazy *fershlooginer* President you
call that a foreign policy ha I'll show you a foreign policy, and
gout, and more melons in heaping array, and taxes. Morris
leaps up from the table. I witness this through a screen door:
Morris leaps heavily *onto* the table. "I've seen it spelled out
by the caraway seeds in the rye! My friends,
go home, be good to those we claim we love. The line between
the sky and the ocean is more firm than the line between
a man's skin and eternity!" Then I back away from the screen.
It grows opaque with the distance. Fog rolls in, and soup steam.
Thirty years ago. (A shrug.) My Uncle Morris Shapiro.

Steerage

*. . . inferior below-decks accommodations on a ship: by
extension, the whole of a certain kind of immigration as the
poor experienced it*

By now, the satchel's leather has reclaimed its living redolence,
it riles at the hasp, and reaching inside it is entering
up past the wrist in the vault of an animal body. Here

they are, in the various tea and fecal colors
of early photography: my grandparents, carrying everything
Europe crammed in a single bag. This

bag. Clumsily held on his shoulder, like a hod, perhaps
to ease an earlier posture. Waiting. One of the first of the lines,
I think—the oily air of the ship's pit still on their faces: it

may be the only thing reproduced here in the original hue.
So now this satchel has its miniature replica floating inside
its belly: a strange idea, vaguely canopic,

soul-like, or homuncular—eldritch, at least. They're
eldritch too, on the dock in their Cracow woolens: little
people, 3, 4 inches, yes, look: I can hold them in my palm

like in the stories. The wee folk. The thumblings. Everywhere,
these old ones, the root ones, have their stories, and
gain strength as the dusk along the woods duff deepens:

menehunes, filing through gates of Hawaiian guava, mango,
for a moment their eyes like budding fruit
the moon lights in the lavish branches; brownies,

kaukases, domovniks, pukys (our Puck) . . . the global
elvish, faces fresh as a thimble-diameter of cream
or puckered like overbathed toes. The nisse, the deive,

the forthright English sprite . . . with their credos,
their language, and their acorn-color aprons or radiant
cobweb negligees . . . every night, through the portals, from their

great ancientdom, into the settlements we've made
the planet's governing order. Darkness
is their steerage; and in it they enter that order,

comprehending or not, however best they can. We
all do. I remember (I was maybe 5, I barely came up
to the bathroom doorknob) tumult over my father's

failed attempts at happily sorting family business
in the files of City Hall. Some long, grandparently
problem, I guess now: rights to property, or citizenship,

who knows? I watched the man who fed me,
flung me, beat the neighbor hound away, walk
dwindling into a building the size of an ocean liner and

walk out hours later looking simply used up. Because
we're little—people born into a giant's land
of bureaucratic backrooms and, beyond it, the universe

stacking matter and antimatter—we have these secret
handshakes, satchels of family heirlooms, private songs . . .
whatever it takes to personalize and console. He

was shaving. I stood by the bathroom door and watched
him suds the mug, then tauten the grain of his neck.
He didn't know I was there. He whistled,

that tune *his* father whistled. Maybe it made the whole damn
day wash away. I think I could whistle it too, a goofy
old world melody—by which we mean there are some of us who

have heard a music that's not of this world.

A Florid Story

That butcher apron stood on its own
—a work day done, the whole of hematology's
spectrum sunk in its fibers, sculpturally.
It came off like a suit of armor's breastplate;
and some huckster who had trudged up all
five flights one night to try to ooze them
into buying con-game English lessons, once
mistook it for a firescreen. In those days

work was 60-hour weeks—*you* figure the hundreds
of lopped-off goose heads, scarlet marbled
rounds of buttcut ox as smooth and continented
as schoolroom globes! When Itzy brought it
home he was bringing home History's coat-of-arms:
fresh red, on a field of old red. And when
Tesseleh laundered, humming in the suds
this cloth tinged tearose pink, when

Tesseleh, bless her, wrung, then scrubbed the rough
pugnacious stains remaining with scouring ash,
and swashed and wrung again, and madly dabbed
with an ammonia sponge for luck, then
finally hung that lavishee of her labor with more
hums, hopeful, weekly, on the line the wash
besplendored in an otherwise-gray space between
two tenements . . . So what? its florid story

might be lighter but could still be read.
The angels in most tales have no sex;
but ghosts are heavy with the pendula and swells
of their originating bodies, are the mannikinish

49

flags of life, and float in air in bondage
to the earth—so laundry, *real* laundry,
never nulls the past, but is a text by which we
save it in its true shape. I say "real"

meaning—what? It's this, I think: the rich
will never know a clothesline. But in neighborhoods
where drying means the look of sails billowing . . .
a boy could walk through such a fleet,
could sit inside its shadows, that make swaying dark
belowdecks. He's heard horrors of how Grampa Itzy voyaged
here in just this way. The word was "steerage," your
clothes were licey, stank, and stuck in your crevices . . .

Soft fossils of us. These
crease-sienna'd cotton briefs and filmy sherbet slips
are ways to read our past, and might imply some commonplaces
work as esperanto. We'll never know Etruscan, already
a mystery tongue by the lifetime of Christ. And even
so, association lets us see a man, perhaps the very
one Augustus Jandolo saw excavated, "a warrior youth
in full military armor," who "the touch of air turned

dust," but once he walked a city's torch-cast shadows,
shift done, cursing an officer (*chickendick!*), gnawing
off an arm of salted cuttlefish for supper-on-the-run,
bone-weary and mean. Beneath his metal leaves,
of course, he's as fragile as anyone. A mother loves him,
cares to take the soilage from his greaves and see it
as tender. And I see *her:* at the stream. She's

humming now, she's pummeling it in the brutal and gentle water.

Coin

When the surgeons slit into my father they went to Jupiter
they went so far, to a barren red moon of Jupiter's.
I'd never been there. My mother had never been there
in him, to a cave on that moon, to the runaway vein
that snaked some inner wall. And even this they slit
and entered, with their geiger counters that fit in a pore.
They needed to hear its half-life keening wildly. There's
one red anti-meson in everyone—here, at this, even
they stopped. Here, at this, my father turned them back,
as all of us were turned back, and he stayed
—as everybody stays, no matter the opening up—
alone in his pain. The microlasers won't usher you there;
or love. In everybody, there's this final landscape
only capable of supporting a population of one.
I was thinking of this as the bus pulled up,
the last bus of the night, at the hospital stop.
It must have been the amber window squares of buslight
in the 3 a.m. pit-dark—I saw that painting of the 18th century
doctorpharmacist Michael Shuppach, studying
a beaker of a patient's urine, meditating, empathizing,
making the late Swiss afternoon light do great
disclosing swirls around that honey and its sediment,
more intimate in ways with this woman than any
deep sexual splitting-apart or any kneeled confessional
admission . . . down to the single citron valence-of-her,
in its nakedness, in his crystal. There's
one golden anti-meson in a life; and here, even he stopped.
There was only one passenger riding the bus: one face
staring out of a window. Someone
needing a bus at 3 a.m. with a story of why
—for a second, before I stood to board and then

decided not to board, our eyes met,
starting a common exchange. —Then
the face shut like a change purse, over
its single coin minted on Jupiter.

Sentimental

The light has traveled unthinkable thousands of miles to be
condensed, recharged, and poured off the white white pages
of an open Bible the country parson holds in front of this couple
in a field, in July, in the sap and the flyswirl of July
in upper Wisconsin, where their vows buzz in a ring in the air
like the flies, and are as sweet as the sap, in these rich and
      ritual minutes.
Is it sentimental? Oops. And out of that Bible the light continues
to rush as if from a faucet. There will be a piecrust cooling
out of its own few x'ed-out cuts. And will it make us run
for the picklier taste of irony rolled around protectively on
      our tongues
like a grab of Greek olives? My students and I discuss this
slippery phenomenon. Does "context" matter? Does
"earned" count? If a balled-up fidget of snakes
in the underbrush dies in a freeze is it sentimental? No,
yes, maybe. What if a litter of cocker spaniels? What
if we called them "puppydogs" in the same poem in that same hard,
hammering winter? When my father was buried,
the gray snow in the cemetery was sheet tin. If I said
that? Yes, no, what does "tone" or "history" do
to the Hollywood hack violinists who patiently wait to play
the taut nerves of the closest human body until from that
lush cue alone, the eyes swell moistly, and the griefs
we warehouse daily take advantage of this thinning
of our systems, then the first sloppy gushes begin . . .
Is that "wrong"? Did I tell you the breaths
of the gravediggers puffed out like factorysmoke
as they bent and straightened, bent and straightened,
mechanically? Are wise old (toothless) Black blues singers
sentimental?—"gran'ma"? "country cookin'"? But

they have their validity, don't they, yes? their
sweat-in-the-creases, picking up the lighting
in a fine-lined mesh of what it means to have gone through time
alive a little bit on this planet. Hands shoot up . . . opinions . . .
questions . . .   What if the sun wept? the moon? Why, in the face
of those open faces, are we so squeamish? Call out
the crippled girl and her only friend the up-for-sale foal,
and let her tootle her woeful pennywhistle musics.
What if some chichi streetwise junkass from the demimonde
gave forth with the story of orphans forced through howling storm
to the workhouse, letting it swing between the icy-blue
quotation marks of cynicism—*then?* What if
I wept? What if I simply put the page down,
rocked my head in my own folded elbows, forgot
the rest of it all, and wept? What if I stepped into
the light of that page, a burnished and uncompromising
light, and walked back up to his stone a final time,
just that, no drama, and it was so cold,
and the air was so brittle, metal buckled
out song like a bandsaw, and there, from inside me,
where they'd been lost in shame and sophistry
all these years now, every last one of my childhood's
heartwormed puppydogs found its natural voice.

Why I Believe in Ghosts

because I've seen the lush brocade,
the nebulae, the Turkish rug imbroglios and rose beds
in the dander rising
up from the hide of a flea-ass village dog in Jocotítlan,
seen the sun inside it
light a dense meadow out of the air, and
through it ran some essence of dog, some
ancestor Dog-of-All-Dogs, absolutely
clear for a moment then gone,
like one of those children's puzzles where you have to find
how many hounds are hiding in this picture and
you look up to show it to Daddy who
was here and now he's
where is he now

———————

because I've seen the musculature
inside a flayed horse carcass and up through its delicate throat
to where the mane was ringleted
repeat
in the grain up a violin's body and scrolled neck
so I know there are levels of ever-tinier
animals and music
and a level below and
below that
and a freeing, at the end, of the final
beast inside
and of the final note

———————

because we all have unfinished business

———————

cecil's missing hand is unfinished business:
his hook is a question mark that never relents
/and Judith wakes some nights and screams:
betrayal in a marriage is unfinished business
/and I have seen, some afternoons on the anniversary
of my father's death, the dust
disturbed by my own slow path
through the Moghileff Brotherhood Cemetery
float low over the ground like a bottle,
at least as translucent as old glass,
maybe more opaque than that, float
like a bottle, in a definite shape,
as if it couldn't settle until
its message was delivered

Vigil

A flower.
          Then the flower
in a book about a flower.
                              How
they double-expose,
                    first one
in the focus of "here"
                        with the other in "almost-here,"
and then the reverse
                    —our one brain working
this binary world
                  together as best it can

—————

—which is a chiefmost lesson
from the "new physics": everything's something else,
enormous empty spaces with occasional particles
moving through a plane on which time is vibration. This
could make a rose a wasteland (highly organized,
of course)
          and still
I'm going to set one, simply and with faith
in its cohesion, at my mother's bedside.
When she moans I'm going to ring for the nurse.
I'm going to push that button as if it's really here,
as if somebody really exists at its other, invisible end,
and really cares there. I'm going to sit in the circle
this pain creates around itself in ever-diminishing power
away from its center, I'm going to sit here all night
with the damp cloth and the lotion,

I'm going to watch and not sleep, I'm going to see
how actual, how solid, I can think of her pain as being
for me as it must be for her.
I'm going to watch as it blossoms.

———————

When I was 10 I thought that aspirin
absorbed the hurt, like tiny sponges. This made hurting
something quantifiable, a thin pernicious liquid
oozing out of the body's most traitorous cells.
30 years later that theory still seems sound enough.
I watch her drowse and weakly toss.
I watch the little damp eked at the corner of her mouth
collect the little light of my reading lamp.
I read and I watch, and I watch as if it
could be efficacious.
                    I read: the new physics
explains, the observer and the observed are never separate.
They exist, they must and they always exist, in a field
of mutuality. Well then, I'm going to watch
until another day is completely lived through.
The new physics says, there are no 2 identical objects.
Not roses—not pennies, for instance.
Their molecules are different molecules, yes
and their submolecular cathedral vaulting and sewerage conduits:
different. Even 2 pennies minted one right after the other.
I'm going to look at this ancient Roman coin
of a vaccination mark struck in her arm
until its irreplaceable face comes alive in the first touch of morning.

The Whole Earth Catalogue

Plate tectonics: like blackened pieces
of sweet pork crackling, the continents slide
on their underside greases. Night; outside,
the sad moon drags the sea behind, a washerwoman
her bucket. The moon
and her crimp-rimmed craters.
The maestro moon and her ever-attentive
oyster castanet orchestra. The atmosphere
of Earth weighs, oh, 5,000
million million tons but a ladybug
bears it untroubled, and

I'm stroking Skyler's back,
the rolling fold between her shoulders,
down the serial rings of the spine and
up again, just lightly, up
and down, and

70 billion neutrinos pass through our bodies
this moment and every moment
and through the lava and through the iron core.
The moon and her purely cosmetic light.
That skyhigh silversmith plating us sterling.
At the vent slits of the Mid-Atlantic Ridge
are sea worms 10 feet long
with no eyes, mouth or gut. And
there are shards of stone with
ferns inside so it looks as if Time is
waiting to be unzipped and entered. And

I'm beside Skyler, almost not touching
her eyelids and her trusting
upturned wrists, but touching them,
figure 8-ing them spiderily with my fingers.
In some Paul Klee

watercolors, as in certain Chinese landscape scrolls,
abstracted hills and sky fill space
to the edges, and it's only
on a second look we see
a minuscule man or a woman is one stroke
of deliberation dabbed in a corner,
going about its own
important business—maybe

setting up, for all we know, an easel for an afternoon
of landscape painting. Getting
the serpent of wind in the wheat
just right. The dusk
rum-coloring the chalk cliffs. Then the moon.
Anchovies gleaming like a miser's hoard
beneath the moon. The moon
and her two Martian stepsisters.
Moon in the rain forests,
moon in the arctic ice, and
mayflies stippling air, and elk
switchbacking eluding pursuing wolves, and
kelp in drift, and galaxies in drift, and

Skyler drifting to sleep, her nipples
tucked under my thumbs, and then the whorled
availability of an ear until she's under. You know

the Eskimo of Greenland voyaged with beautiful
carvings always in their canoes,
a foot long, maybe 18 inches. They look like
spinal columns of angels or troll lords, long
and knobbed and coved. They're maps
of several hundred miles of the coastline
most worth knowing. They fondled them over
and over. On nights with no moon,
in such dark there's no planet,
the eyes in their fingers knew these by heart.

Others

. . .

and in the twilight the sound comes up
across the neighborhood backyards of a table
being set. Other lives with other schedules.

—ROBERT HASS,
"Santa Barbara Road"

A Letter

Number of direct-mail solicitations sent to Henry David
Thoreau at Walden Pond this year: 90.
       —Harper's Index, 1988

At the end of a day that's rubble around me,
shrimp husks, tufts on a barber's floor, heaped circus doo,
at the burr tail-end, the tar tail-end,
the shitty piggy corkscrew tail-end of a day like that,
when all the dauby, wadded toilet paper staunchings of the shaving
  mistakes
of a lifetime buzz about this air like ghost wasps,
and to try to even say a word like *graciousness* or *honor*
coughs a bile-larded furball up into the throat . . .
at the end of a day like that, I pick you up,
Old Chisel-Puss, and head out to the last, thin brothlight
just to read some random observation you whittled,
cleansed in lime and ashes, then set on your simple sill
for the world to do as it will with it, yes,
Henry David, Old Man Applemash, Hardwood Grainface, you.
I like sometimes to take rank hold on life and spend my day
more as the animals do. You don't fail me
now and never have, Old Clear Clean Vinegar Eye.
There is no odor so bad as that which arises from
goodness tainted. Old Man Aphorism, Duke of Bean Rows, here
the lowered sun behind a lowered cloud rays out
in the shape of a clamshell—you
of all the boneyard might in one quick strike convince me
this is a delicious evening, when the whole body is one sense
and imbibes delight through every pore. Eventually
it's night, a little pearly murk and then the real
anthracite thing. This far into the blotto glow of the city,
there aren't many stars—enough, though,

for a small game of Commemorative Dot-to-Dot.
I'd like to place you among them: you'll shine
like a chart of the major nerve-ends.
I'd like to place you among them and ask you to peer down
once a night with your acerbic, well-intentioned gaze.
The horoscope zoo grunts, caterwauls, and burbles up there
uselessly—we could use some understanding
astral attention. I'd like to place you among them
just so we could point on cloudless nights: there's
Old Sufficience himself, the Scraggled Dour Lover of Stuff,
the Great Denouncer, Mr. Stickler, that Saint of Cheapskates
and Wonderful Phoney-Baloney of the Woods, the Lone Looker
who said *Every man has to learn the points of the compass again
as often as he wakes.* Who said *Olympus is but
the outside of the earth every where.* I'd like to constellate you
overhead. Don't tell me you wouldn't be pleased.
This far into the blotto glow of the 20th century,
your light isn't strong—but it's enough. I'm 40.
When I was 10, I wished on those stars. Oh
they might have been dead, but we corresponded.

Homage

        In
the fin-
        icky world of that small bright-
colored attendant
        of the sides of trout,
the cleaner-wrasse, an interscale precision
means everything. Here's one, pendant
        near a gill, and going minutely about
the business of dining on some parasitic mite.
As wrasse lips sup along trout skin
        a lovely fish-to-fish elision
occurs: one groomed, one fed, fin-

        esse
as tes-
        tament to a unit larger than *it* is.
        When I eat you
        in bed, that rich, mulch, human-
fish taste coursing through, I feel
as if I become—and complete—you
        in a roughly similar way; so the numin-
ous, sloppy, unboundaried sexual bliss
is also built of tinier exactitudes: es-
        trogen levels, shared ease, and the peel-
ing back of the clitoral sheath that means *yes.*

        Ho-
cus po-
        cus much more actual than my "I be-
        come you" (refer
            above) occurs in the wrasse's

coral garden world. Each is born female. Each's
place is as a female flashing in a shoal one bur-
   ly male leads. She grows. She passes
up in rank. And should the male disappear, the fe-
male closest in size may take completely o-
   ver, changing sex—as if she reaches,
through some larger blur, a focus. So

      sure-
ly lur-
      id a transformation (on the human plane) is here
      (the piscine) ordinary
         and beautiful. As we study
a slim gold loaf of wrasses elegantly fan
out in a wedge, then spiral, a lemon peel of very
      serpentine twist, then close again in muddy
regrouping, we see the hugeness we're
a part of relies on its every component's being as pure-
      ly exact as it can. As she was—Marianne
Moore.

Shawabty, Ushabi, or *Shabti* Figures

Some are lumpish terra-cotta cylinders little more human
than bud vases. Others are gem-set
gold over detailed cedar musculature. The afterlife was life
continuing heightened—there would be groves of palm
belonging to the gods, and date, and lotus, requiring
heightened care. So these would represent
the deceased, these were obliged by magic text
and contract: *O shabtis go quickly to work*
with their inch hoes shouldered like muskets, inch
irrigation-picks, inch plows *Say "we are ready."*
One deed of sale (not rare) is for a set of 365 shabtis
"and their thirty-six overseers, all: 401, to my satisfaction."
In Mesopotamia, statues worshipped the gods nonstop for
    their owners.
In Tut's tomb they found 1,866 separate fine-toothed inch tools.

TV tonight: a pseudo-documentary on Coleridge. Just
now he's enlisted in the 15th Light Dragoons,
a cavalry unit, although he sneezes near horses and
can't ride fifteen yards. Kerosening the dung-tubs clean,
he sets his clothes on fire. He upchucks supper so
dependably, it's requested he dine in the stables.
Saddles fly off. Swords snap. Whole cannon collapse.
So they allow his brothers to "buy him out"—that is,
purchase a substitute. You could do that then. They
eye each other a moment, then a commercial comes on . . .
The gofer wheeling in lunch, the set's vet checking
the wire-tripped horses, "Coleridge" resting behind a door
marked *Star* while the dangerous scenes are done with,
his stunt-man wrapping up good in asbestos.

Pheletos of Cos

*Isn't there any heaven where old beautiful dances, old
beautiful intimacies prolong themselves? Isn't there any
Nirvana pervaded by the faint thrilling of instruments
that have fallen into the dust of wormwood . . .*

—FORD MADOX FORD

That was the year we attended the Karl Janifer concert
a half-mile off the coast. Whatever lazy jam
developed on the causeway, the island itself
—spring-green, almost perfectly round, with the small rise
in its center and the single mock-Tudor trustee's house
on that—was worth all jostle. Only later, I mean
by years, when we were having the final argument
over the mortgage and its accumulated weight, did I see
how it started back then, a thousand miles away,
on the porch where Janifer hit the first irreproachable
chord of his solo piano performance exactly,
to the second, as the sun disappeared. It was silent
(500 people on blankets like ripples around
the house, and it was silent), there was a last
matchflame-sized straggle of light, and then
the horizon took it, and Janifer charged the new
blue air with his chord. Of course we were
exalted. The keys were the white and black stripes
of a zebra stampede, the keys were the mile-eating
ties of the great New Wave Jazz Railroad. There
was only a minute or two, out of maybe three hours,
when some of the ambience-orchestration failed:
an unaccounted-for wind off the shore rocks
stole a passage out of the air, as cleanly
devastating as a wrecking crew's scoop.
A minute or two, no more—then return to the quiet

continuing melody-line, the wine, the gradual hot-bodied
clarification of the stars. But back at Sandy's
wasn't it just that momentary loss we
wondered over till sunrise—the five of us: where
did it go to, that passage? Into the wind, yes.
Into the unseen sexual center in the tightly furled
invisible rose of the wind. Into the dust of the wind,
the pollen of the wind: the grains of time
in an hourglass sized to the life of a galaxy.
Into the vast, voluted, museumly wind,
where the gone are pressed in eternal display
in the spaces between wind-nuclei. The Tudorish house,
though, seemed stable. Maybe it's still there, I
wouldn't know. I know that Sandy's dead
—her last hours hooked to the tubes went slow but easy.
And I know it's a fear of going with
that passage, that makes the things of a life
accumulate. The solids, a house, a coterie,
the thousand-and-one commitments. These
are the ongoing days of garden hose and contract,
milkglass vase collection heavily insured and credit renewal,
poundage, welcome mat, fatness and rooting. Pheletos of Cos,
the dwarf grammarian and poet, was said
to be so small he needed weighting himself with stones
or else the wind would abduct him. Maybe
he should have gone—wherever. Maybe he should
have gone, come back to us, and reported on that place
where the music is carried to, so we'd know
at last if the piling of stones is worth it. We
could ask, then . . . but I see him in his two
components, stone and wind, wind and stone,
which make of him a horizon. Every time
we take a step near with the question, he
moves a step back and the answer is lost.

The History of Buttons

A trivial case is the history of buttons: there are
few events. An example of excessive factuality is the
textbook on the whole history of world art, which
must embrace all the principal events from paleolithic
painting to the present. Somewhere between triviality
and factuality lie the sequences we are seeking.

　　　　　　　　　　　　　　　　—Arranged from
　　　　　　　　　　　　　　　　GEORGE KUBLER

1.

Night's first weak sheets
are drifted over the sun. It's 6 p.m. By 7,
something more than sootiness—a hint
of the original, Big Bang ink of things—
is in the sky, uncertain
of its fit. By 8, a full moon
firmly fastens it.

　　　　　　　　This

　　　　　———————

is the time of objects, even bodies, giving definition
back. I watch you enter sleep, white pill
night starts to dissolve
in its system. —Me? awake,

　　　　　　　　　　　　I'm disappearing
as well, down a funnel of reading.
It's night here too. No,
a cave. And then beginning licks of fire
rolling smokily over the great painted creatures,
bison as sturdy as maps of a continent,
deer, fish, ripplefoliate deer and ripplefoliate fish,
the bulls as bulky yet graceful as hills come to life,

and painted from those same hills' ochers. This
is the magic time when things, the first things
—scraper, smasher, clasper—gather
out from abstraction. This is the time
of the bearing of bones, the first, enormous, hill-bull
bones, to their first moments of yielding
smaller nouns. This pouring beast on the floor
being smashed, being scraped—and this one
bone-white button Renoir has given Madame Renoir
on her blouse, in his pinks, and sardine grays, and ambers.
It's placed so . . . if you unbuttoned it,
everything unbuttons, the canvas, the space she completes.
Her buttery breasts tumble into your palms
on the crest of the first rush
forward of the history of art.

2.

And then the artist sets aside his tubes
that were curled like a dinner of fresh shrimp
on a folding tray; the light of the studio
dies. But the light of physics goes on
unthinkably, it curves time, it
goes all the way to where there's God or no God
then loops back and doesn't
care what it holds and it holds everything,
and physics says in places light can untie like a knot,
sink backwards into itself, and undo down
to units the mad couldn't see or the seraphim tally . . .
Spend a night alone with such intangible conundrum,
with neutrinos and The Void, you'll be de-moted
truly: just another grain of dust
freefloating cosmic thermals.
You could be a man who knows enough to know
the skin of anything is mainly empty space, a little
subatomic rhumba, mainly empty space,

so you could fall forever
through yourself without touching a single
demonstrable thing . . .
                              except for the buttons
in Rembrandt's *Anatomy Lesson of Doctor Joan Deyman*.
I count 15, in a tidy run
down the front of the surgeonphysician's gown,
descending (for he backs
the propped cadaver) into the slit
in the braincase itself. The corpse's
soles loll at us like butchershop hams.
The chest is sawed and emptied, and
that portion of its walls we watch
is densely textured, slippery, rib-corrugated.
The nipples are gabled stiff.
Well, if it horrifies, it does so
in reminding us the body *is* a solid,
                                        and
in Clara Tice's lithe erotic watercolor
Mademoiselle de Maupin, we can see the kneeling dandy
lifts his mistress's sex to his lips like a chalice:
he's one deep drink. It balances
the Rembrandt by its life-ripe pastels, yes; but
also by its being a body naked and a body clothed,
in interarchitecture. She
is such a flushed expanse of pleasure we shudder, and
her breasts' peaked centers are more themselves
for his frock coat's 2 back buttons.

3.
Madame Renoir is skinning a peach, is ribboning
this stripping into one unbroken spiral that,
like any watchspring, winds up some of the future.
Marbling river-light is mysterious
over her neck and over her arms and over the very silly

74

filament of loose hair curled like a fiddlehead at her nape.
And even sillier is when she delivers
the pit from between her teeth—it glistens there,
a something prehistoric offered up on her tongue.
She laughs; it makes the blouse look like striped light
being run through by animals. And then,
quite simply, she places the damp, deep-tourmaline pit
off-center on a shining linen napkin, and
the planet's afternoon adjusts, by fractions
of color and structure, to
accommodate this weighting . . .   The
                                        "events,"
as Kubler calls them, the "events" are what
we make of them and choose to call a history;
the rest is undifferentiated
time. In buttons, these are the epochs:
bangers, nickers, sinkeys, shankeys, bird's eyes,
baskets, honeycombs, old dorsets, liveries,
singletons, crosswheels, death's heads, goofies, orient swirls.
This is the drama: highway robbers
carrying razors especially to "bubble," i.e.
slash the buttons from, their victims.
This is the story of diamond; of sheep horn.
These are the "5 Traditional Chinese Buttons":
Justice, Humility, Order, Prudence, Rectitude. And
this is the "first" "true" button rising
out of Danish Iron Age peat, where bogweight has kept it
entire, and bogweight has kept its ancient wearer
young. Her skin is like lacquered paper.
We know her last meal—the belly, eloquent
after 300 years. The tiny lines
fanned from the corners of her eyes are dark like tarnish
over pattern that's readable still. She says
what Deyman's gutted meat-of-a-man says
too, though the saying sounds witlessly simple: this

is what we are, when what we also are
is gone. At 3 a.m. it means
                    a man should close a book,

———————

come snuggle next to you, and love what there is
in a living surface, love what it means to be here
at the end of uncountable miles of lacelike nerve,
lung-lining, nephron tubule, snaggled delicate
blood we see fronded through eyes, here
where our days with each other
hang by their precious, hang by their pitiful, threads.

Los Verdados & After & Long After

1.

Bernie, goes the story, toppled whapped as if by a 2 x 4
nose-first in his serving of refried beans and *tacos
al carbon*—but whapped from inside; Guy,
whose slack command of Spanish provided in crisis only
puta and *soy Americano*, ran off the terrace and through
the village twists in panic, finally wringing *Mi amigo!
Corazón malado! Help!* from some bilingual brain-thread,
and in time—in, that is, village Mexico no-time, its
metabolism that of sedimentary rock—*los médicos*
arrived and gurneyed the patient away, his nose
in profile capped by a miniature coronet
of lard-in-large-part bean goop. Now I tell you this

half-comically about whole pain because the particulars
float that tone as if condoning it—even so,
the ruddy glow of Bernie's face was drained to the whey
and veiny colors of bleu cheese in a second, and Guy saw how
pathetically thin is the string of being-alive that waggles
through our adiposal selves. The next day found him back
at the local and only *cantina*, surveying its local and
only no-choice fare: the beans, the gray-laced pork,
and a side dish vaguely like olives in puddled-up cheese with
some sebaceous substance pseudopoding out the scrim. He
couldn't eat. And in the next few days was too on the
go. "It's how Mexico functions," that's all: bribing

this suave clinic functionary for visits, that
nurse known otherwise for her torpor, brushing *dinero*
like oleo over the palms of half, it seemed, the adult population. If
the greed of the few or the poverty of the countless were its cause,

he couldn't figure—and didn't have time: when they
unwrapped that fatty glut from Bernie's ticker they
rewrapped his case in red tape, and it finally took
a mattress-stash of Mexican moola to bag up Bernie (this is
true) as a side of beef intended for the clinic's anniversary dinner,
rolling him muttering under his breath down the halls
on a food cart, every paid-off face turned nonchalantly
izquierda or *derecha*. This is not to defame

2.
a place or its culture. Back in the States, both
gringos agreed that neither colonnaded Halls of Justice nor
the normally agglutinizing diner repasts of their native
Philly differed from Los Verdados in kind, but differed
only in working up subtler expression. This is all
sloshed willynilly in my noggin as I sit here glumly
in Wichita, Kansas, watching my crankcase drained
and various obscure parts that look like robots' earbones
screwed professionally in, after being special-ordered from
somewhere called The Factory, after a cool green 5 slipped
quick as a glug of unction from my hand to my mechanic's and
I was magically lifted to first in line. It's Bernie

all over: the tapping of oil, the sweet shush of cash, the ministering
technicians. I can see the touch of his horrible story
everywhere, suddenly. Edie's courtship is "on the rocks,"
which I thought meant wrecked, like a ship, but learn is
bourbon after bourbon in Herb's study after dark; she
buys him back from that deep amber stupor with sex "not
that he can manage by then" and weeps afraid one day her curves
will lose to the staunch silhouette of the bottle. "After fucking
like that I feel . . . it's like a used car salesman's hair slick
coats me all over." But—does she love him?: yes. He, her?:
yes. Love love love, my friends. Our hearts won't stop
attacking. And Bernie, who nuzzled with Death—what

wisdom draggeth he back? "It was a one-night stand,
m'boy; I didn't *marry* her." So there. If we believe the Word
as Swedenborg received it, Heaven is shade-tree streets with
porches and a 6-pack, just like here, except it's
Always. That was what they thought in Egypt, and you know
those plow, cosmetic dish, fish net, and inlaid scribe board
figurines were true tools for the Afterlife—provisions. If
it really is the same there, then I recommend the Chinese idea
of "hell money"—bills, in large denominations, burned
at the loved one's grave. Officialdom being what it is . . .
they take a final touch of this
world's grease to ease the other.

The Children of Elmer

Somewhere as I write this, Cyndi Ybarra, 12, is happy or
thinks she's happy—the men who visit the whorehouse
like her, and attend to her dramas and peevishness,
which is more than her father the big prick ever did, and
when she shows her little trick with the empty chianti bottle
especially, they'll become especially nice, so much that even
the few whose pleasure is hurting, leaving a plum or nectarine
of blood below her skin like the start of a still life, these
will joke with her, one bought her a mint-green parakeet, one
    a t-shirt
with her favorite group her mother once refused buying.
    Her mother,

meanwhile, is on the local news each night for a week
imploring. They have a special minute-long spot now,
"Disappearances"—the "last-seen-wearing . . . ," the tears,
the classroom photograph . . .   In this night's picture: 17
6th-graders make a sloppy line for "milk break." —Which
was bottles once, when I was 12, and I remember
Russell Lupakovich chunking his across the room in
dervish pique (he could also cut a really juicy
fart on request) and to this day I find that absolutely
dazzling streak like a comet across the blackboard

liberating. 27 years and its shatter still thrills. So container
meant glass, and anything else I suppose was
unthinkable. Each 3 days, 6 new milks in a wire basket
at our back door, like an honor guard in uniforms
so otherwordly ivory they swam in the sun.
Eventually everything disappears—that's no especially

oracular wisdom. The next I remember, it's half-quart
cartons with a coat of wax a kid could thickly
scrape up under his nails ("Albie, *don't!*"), a something
sensuous, like picking at a scab—then, pleasures,

even small ones, vanishing over time as if to some law,
the next I know about, the cartons are these joyless things
the most enthusiastic or neurotic amongst us couldn't scrape
a gnat's-ass-worth of wax from. I see Lupakovich
mournfully shaking his gog-eyed kettledrum head (that
he could really play with sticks, too) at this loss, as now
he's lost to me in the clutter of what years do, and Emmylou
Baker who thought I was cute and had her period in gym
is lost, and Eddie "Pitface," and Moe, and . . .   wasn't there a
        girl named
Ybarra? I think so. She'd be a mother by now . . .   This

roll call of lost children makes me crazed for securing the child
I was—in science fiction they'll travel back blotting the past, so
then the present goes up in a puff of smoke; I'm frightened.
I work all night, and find him: adam's apple, canvas shoes, he's
at the "ice chest" for a chocolate milk. Its famous
dairy character, Elsie the Cow. She's married to stolid Elmer.
Here, she's walking—high heels and matronly apron—with
"milk products" on a silver platter. Hooray! Their boy-girl
        calves dance.
No one strays, or ever cares to, from this house's
model clarity—which I believed in truly and aspired to

for years. Well, now it's 1987. And it's dark. Obsidian
dark. It's 4 a.m., and as I write this in the house
I live alone in, I can hear the kitchen faucet titrate
in to the darkness by drops, can see the pilot light in its almost
parental vigil. The refrigerator hums—bravado. I

open her up, and turn the cold to high; as if . . .   Now Elsie's
gone. These cartons are a gallery of the missing: Teddy Maeloff,
7; Duberry Jackson, 15; Elisha Jolene MacGurdy, 10.
. . . as if I were the guardian of those small stamped
expiration dates. As if I could preserve them.

The Alias: A Survey

You aren't you. You're sleeping. Now your bones are
marionettesticks in a dark heap, waiting morning.
We can't help but be to time this way as chameleons are
to color. In their world, degrees of the globe to the east,
the cells in the wild lime skin of one are dials tuning in
a tame rock-gray; another's a flower by now,
in a convocation of flowers wearing the deep carnelian robes
of authority and a golden anther crown. Nearby, a turtle
belly's a witch doctor's mask. A worm's the crest
of a tongue some fish lure other fish with. A john

could be a dog ("You're a dog," she says) at the feet
of a whore in dominatrix latex. "Lick my boots,"
she says, and "Wouldn't my little doggie like a pussy
to play with," and "Bark for it then." And then
he leaves—he's Boss at the office, Daddy at home, and
Honey Bear in bed that night for a reason that's none
of my snoopy poet's business or yours, though in that
dark, we all know, wives can lightly stroke their husbands' eyes
like field anthropologists who think they really understand
the whole of a culture behind its ceremonial masks. Who

knows? The gods have spoken through a court dwarf
tranced by candles, through a burly hulk out hauling
geese in from traps when he thinks he sees "a sign"
—and spoken alike. Through spots the size and indigo-purple
of grapes, on a raw ram's liver. Through trees. Through
seizures. Through little idols sculpted from horn.
Through some of our skulls like an off-duty medic being
beeped to emergency business. The radar marker sweeps

around a weather-scope and it's only another oracle of the one
true universe showing us her folds. If a goose did

land in a baited field, frighten, and fly, the feather
left behind might enter the life of a tip kept ready
every day in a crystal well of ink—the former life of a tip
implanted in the quick amino acids of a living bird would be
its long-gone homeland. If an author lifts a quill to write
a credible novel of espionage, he'll use a *nom de plume*
—you have to be careful. One expatriate double-agent
disguised as a birder paces the city park, and waits
for the operative only known as The Clown to bike up
whistling. Across the street from the park, the dominatrix

—her name is Lucy—is home at last, and brusquely pulls
        the curtains
closed to all of this. For a while she watches their green batiste
weave ripples from the sun. Then she goes to her father's
darkened room. She thinks she can actually smell the
cancer. The arm that's left is as spare as a scepter; he
raises it, with a tired aplomb, admitting her. And then of
course the long routine of soiled pads and prescriptions. By
the time she's done, the livingroom curtains are gray. She
hates it. A late bird calls in the park, then stills. Her bourbon
lowers. She eases back to his room and sees

sleep make his face into someone she loves.

"Too Much,"

a friend says inevitably when circumstance tickles his
wonderment bone. So, following the story of the starlet
and the hardboiled eggs, or the palmed duck liver
a psychic healer claimed was a tumor
successfully meditated out of a young boy's gut . . .
too much. It comes with a dazed shake of the head
and a hesitant chuckle. "The Human Aquarium"
Mac Norton would swallow six live goldfish and one
dozen frogs, then reproduce them,
"one at a time, from between his lips, head first."
And all alive and keeking, he'd say. Too much.
According to *Guinness,* a Michael Lotito has *eaten* seven
bicycles entirely, and a Cessna plane.

Phil was stationed in Panama, a medic
whose duties included driving their surgery trash
along the isthmus trail to the dump site. "There's
a time in the season they call 'blue wobble.'
Millions of blue crabs migrate, blue that's almost
neon-blue. You don't see ground at all, just miles
of moving blue rollerbelt. They cross
that trail. The jeep crushed thousands easily,
you'd hear the continued wet crackle of it but never
see the bodies, new crabs clambered over too fast. This
sometimes happened: we'd fling the bags in the dump bin,
then stare slackfaced a moment. One would hiss
or raise its claw. And we'd be out of the jeep with wrenches,
smashing them, smeared in it, crazed from the numbers."

Too much isn't the felled tree, or the company's
eight-car train of trees in the mill lot, it's
one palomino-color shaving spiraling as delicate
as a pubic curl from the whittler's stick;
it's one iron filing my eye-film snagged and
my mother dabbed out with her own damp tongue.
How much did it snow that winter, '61, when
I was thirteen, raw with thirteen, and one flake,
I felt, could explode me? Paths out
were catacombs; quarries filled, in just over an hour.
And my parents left, supposedly to grocery shop but
really to bicker "not in front of the boy"
—snowed in so far past being hard on each other, it
packed them into an icy ball.

If I had 2¢ for every poem I've written or read
with lovers' spats embittering it, I'd be 200
glittering pazoozas nearer let's-retire wealth, but
still couldn't buy back your sweetness tonight. And
though the muddy dump of corpse on corpse
the news unearthed for its viewers this evening is saying
ours is a luxury sadness, and nothing to do with some
babushka'd mama stumbling trying to match
a loose arm held in her arms to a girl's chopped body . . .
still, you cried, I almost cried, and now
your back is turned, a blank screen
for my sleeplessness to complete with home movies
of suffering. How did it happen? who knows? just
a word. You were talking. I threw my 2¢ in.

Give me a villain. Give me just one clearcut targeted
ne'er-do-well with rat eyes and a smoking gun, to hold
responsible all night while the stink of cordite settles.
Well, he isn't here. He never was. It's all of us
torturing all of us. It's dressed in its Sunday best.
And the boy with the tumor? Of course The Great
Shaheesh the Mystic Light was no more help
than the great chemotherapy; now he's barely a doll
of himself. I've watched his mother watch his face
with the sun on it, then with the moon on it, watching
until time had no meaning: we're floating,
falling, yes, and even the unhearable klaxon-horn
of a hadron, the unbroached stroke of a lepton, just a single
neutrino barely in existence's embrace, is too much.

———————

Too much is a remora, like a cyclopean wing,
between your shoulder blades—fluttering, sucking.
Too much calls the shots. Too much sashays
into the party and everyone fumbles to ogle her
nipple knowingly bou-bou-bouncing alongside her gilded
lily corsage. Too much, too much. The sky: too much.
The zillion human endeavors we endeavor to balance out
the sky: too much. Phil says they kept their canteen bowl
of sugar in a larger bowl of water
—like a moat—and yet the ants marched in
and drowned, and more ants over them, that drowned,
and then more ants, until a bridge of ant cadavers
let the ants succeed in reaching the sugar and passing it
back to the ants, and so on, to the jungle.

———————

We wake: a junco, a power saw, and a neighborkid's
remorseless skateboard stitch-and-growl in orchestral
cahoots. Sleep's pretzeled our legs together. Wake:
the sun gold yolk over your hip, the fog
in my body's long corridors thinning. A few
neurochemical windows groan open, remembering, taking
stock of the place. Abundant trouble's waiting out there,
yanking a black brim over its eye and flicking a match.
Your sleepbreath in and out on the pillow. Then your
mouth on my mouth. This easy, Precambrian time
of day, before language. I'm hungry—the orange liqueur
fudge truffles are tinfoiled-up in the fridge, your
consciousful nipple stiff in my lips, the light, the world—
I'm hungry, people, and nothing's enough.

———————

In Boston, on January 15, of 1919, a steel tank
of the Purity Distilling Company burst: and 2.3
million gallons of stored molasses hit the streets
in thirty-foot waves. Hundreds of horses were mired
like flies on flypaper. Twenty-one people died of suffocation,
some still holding their poker hands or their firewood, like
the bodies at Pompeii. Weeks later, its gum still
filmed the trolley seats and doorknobs of that city.
A codger tells us this at the Antiques Fair—he's
selling old Purity Company crocks. "Be careful, *too* much
sweetness, even, ain't good" he winks out
axiomatically, but that's tough to believe. We're
hand in hand today. We've left *Depression Glass* somewhere
behind, and head off for *Fiestaware*.

———————

In the winter of 1961 the snow was . . .
do you remember how deep
the snow was? My parents are clomping home
from grocery shopping, holding their fat bags
easily seven inches above
the silvery tips of car antennae.
Somewhere below, my tuna sandwich is
hardened into a terra-cotta slab
in the Chevrolet's trunk, and might as well be
Ur or Babylon. So, way up there
it's like walking around the future. As always,
the future is barely aware.
They're giggling with each other, and their breaths
run ahead like white minks on a leash.

Spies (*Spies?* Spies.)

1.
are everywhere. / They float,
trenchcoated, slant-capped, from deep cover and code name
into the always unsatisfactory half-revelation
of newspaper headlines. / Ultrasound
sweeps deepness for the human fetus
and Nessie impartially. / First the serpent
reconnoiters Eve—then,
civilizations later, a microtransmitter planted inside
a martini olive reports some woman's pillow-natter
directly to HQ. / Espionage
of telescope and stars, of information-tweezing
priest and confessee, of bug-eyed girl on her knees
at the stark-lit crack in the bathroom door
one night as daddy pees . . . / Let's spy
on me: I'm

———————

7, peering under the ever-braiding skin
of Humboldt Creek and, farther on, the calm
and glutted pond it ruffles into. A duo of chipmunks
cavorts nearby; but I'm near-mesmerized
by the subsurface gulpings of great
handbag-sized fish, as if the car keys,
a kerchief, torn concert tickets, just might
leisurely spiral from those throats and spell
some secret life to the air. Was I
a "spy"? No. Was this "wrong"? No. Though
if I swiveled that same observation 180
degrees, sneak-peeking the hot-stuff couple

grazing each other's necks on a shadowy
park bench—*then?* Was Nixon's
wiretapping "wrong"? He "meant well." Meaning
—what? When I was 17

my father would wait, however long it lasted,
3 in the morning, 4, until my date
(she drove, I didn't yet) pulled softly under
the block's most lushly canopied tree
for a last goofy passionate smooch: and out
of love? concern? sheer nosiness? his
wakeful sentinel eye would burn
from a chink in the livingroom blinds straight
into my teenage brain's overwary
embarrassment center. We'd argue. I'd tell him go
to hell. I'm 41 now, *that's*
what I'm embarrassed over. Yes: it *was* his own
lonely version of love, I think. But
love for me in those crazy hormonal days meant
walking into the house with a fresh fishy smear
of my girlfriend over my mouth—from,
as she'd say (embarrassed
but knowing her needs and their empetaled location)
"down there." Well, that was fine with me,
a novice, a supplicant, someone exploring the mysteries
finely creased in places "down there" even she couldn't guess at yet
—a spy in the valley of love.

2.
The vagina of O'Keeffe's
Gray Line with Black, Blue, and Yellow
is also a flower's
infinitely receding tissuey layers. It's wet
still, done, redone, on one of two easels
this morning in 1953 in Abiquiu. She

studies this painted image—not for content so much
right now, but its overall shape on the canvas.
Beside it, another canvas, with the same shape, but:
a horse skull. She flicks
back and forth and back and forth, while desert light
acts as an awl in her studio, scraping everything
free of the inessential. She's studying likeness
and layers: an espionage of what
ticks at the quick of us. It reminds me of
the Sung Dynasty poet Chiant Te-li's two lines:
Painting plum blossoms is done like judging horses
—By bone-structure, not by appearance.

It reminds the informer
—a "confidential informant of Bureau-proven reliability,"
according to the file—of nothing, duty and bile
blocking anything other than damning-by-implication
reportage: that she "made remarks
which would not be made by a loyal American,"
that "she frequently entertains guests of foreign extraction,"
one even "appeared to be either Chinese or Filipino
and did not speak any English . . ." 1953, and O'Keeffe
is under surveillance
for the FBI office in Albuquerque. A "mail watch"
is placed on her correspondence. Her observer somehow
scrutinizes her bookshelves. Altogether,
117 pages of dossier are amassed toward no particular end
by Hoover's snooping boys. For Dorothy Parker,
1,000 pages. Theodore Dreiser, 240.
Archibald MacLeish, 600+ . . .
The ear against the tapestry of a medieval council-of-war,
and the spy jet thermalphotographing missile installations:
each has its own sensibility, but

I see them as two of endless circles around her
passionate daubing of paint, up to her elbows
in coral, turquoise, burnt sienna, terra verde, dove-gray,
        amethyst, ocher . . .
1953. The orbits of the atom build up
to the rings of the onion, and these are like
the pearly bands in the universe-wall that oversee
the Music of the Spheres; they revolve; and,
surreptitiously, each watches each.

———————

Those two "cavorting chipmunks" . . . ?—mechanical
transmission devices, disguised as living things.
If I unreel their tapes and play back
1955, I see that curious 7-year-old boy being led home
hand in hand, by his curious father. I can even
feel the finger bones in the older one's hand, see?, playing
with the slippery give of knuckle-skin over the knuckles.
And if I follow the tape up
32 more years, I'm cradling his head in my arms
the week before he dies, I'm feeling the hardness
under the delicate skin at the temples, I'm rubbing
pressure-points against the unavoidable skull. O'Keeffe
would understand. But who can understand
those moments when he still appears
over my shoulder now, a sentient
smudge on the oxygen, and noting,
as if they were meaningful, the very confused
particulars of my life? It's like
old times, in a way. It's his own
lonely version of love, I think. The air
goes cloudy . . .   I feel his gaze . . .
Who does he report to?

Physics

. . . the primordial material ("ylem" Gamow called it, after an old Greek word for the substance of the cosmos prior to the evolution of form) . . .

—TIMOTHY FERRIS

12th Century Chinese Painting with
a Few Dozen Seal Imprints
Across It

The tea has given way to plum wine,
and still they're talking, animated down to points
of fire deep in their pupils—two scholars. "Look,"
one motions at what's outside the sliding panels: landscape
where the purling of river leads to foothills,
then to the tree-frowzed mountains themselves, and
up from there . . .   The sky
has opened. Out of it, as large as temple gongs
yet floating as easily as snowflakes, pour
transistor circuits, maps of topiaries, cattle brands,
IUDs, the floorplans of stockades, cartouches,
hibachi grills, lace doilywork, horsecollars,
laboratory mouse-mazes, brain-impressions, all of it
sketching the air like a show of translucent
kites in blacks and reds, a few beginning
("Look, *there* . . .") to snag in the treeline, or hover
above the whorling bunched rush of a riverbend . . .
"You see?" says one with a shrug and eloquent
tenting-up of his eyebrows, "You *see?*"—he's
too polite to declaim it in words.
They've been arguing if The Other World exists.

The Niggling Mystery

The wanton troopers riding by
Have shot my fawn, and it will die.
Now my sweet fawn is vanished to
Whither the swans and turtles go . . .
> —ANDREW MARVELL,
> *The Nymph Complaining*
> *for the Death of Her Fawn*
> (1681)

In my dream of Newton, a great knock
at the great man's great portcullis admits

the giant, tic-eyed, moss-dentitioned captain of the troops:
they have, as per request, delivered the entire

carcass (so fresh, settling flies still pluck
its nerves like a viola) to his gate. Through

some upwelling psyche-pinprick, all
the tumult of my waking day—from browsed

Marvell, to your bruised
look when I invoke old lovers—flummoxed willynilly

into this 17th century sky, the all-revealing
light of which is a perfect cone through the diamonded panes and

holds the cooling animal in specimen-preparedness on
his laboratory slab. He

burns to know. He's sure that with the gleaming tweezers
of his reason (plus some haunch-saws and the calipers)

he'll slice beyond the surface slick of fresh fawn organs,
rainbowsheen heart-casing, pudding brains, past even

the cilia-oared confetti microtenants
of the blood, and find, and formularize for all time,

spectrum-regular and gravity-clasped, whatever niggling
mystery it is in such a beast that makes the poets slobber

breathily, and certain otherwise-stern hunters
grunt and turn aside to hide a weakness. Muscles

fly. What looks like pancreas stroganoff gets tossed
over his shoulder. All of this has been gridded

before him—he wants smaller and deeper. Uterine
vesicles, retinal nubs and sub-nubs, lung grains, mucilloids . . .

until at the last damp pore he exposes a pinprick
that's a black hole in space—it whooshes

anti-matter, tiny alternate universe moons,
through the room: a coin where UFOs and archangels are

tails and heads, one luminous sphere with Buddha
at its gyroscopic center, and a coral cameo brooch of your face

I love, in pain because love means the giving to an Other
of the power exactly to cause pain . . .   I wake as Newton

goes mad. I remember him wearing the raw
fawn head for a mask. And I remember

Anne, a long-ago lover, saying when she was a child,
once, she bundled a newly dead grasshopper

into the house, in a rag, from a curbside puddle.
All of her friends grouped around. She set that ratcheted

geometry on her mother's best lustreware saucer and
then, with strict determination, asking

silence, and as if tranced by spiritmedical
forces beyond her, Anne plied the hinges

between her forefinger and thumb, the pipette insect
drumsticks, pumped until an oily bead

plumped at its jaws, there was a twitch, and then
that jointwork lazarus snapped a leap matched

easily by the children's. They ran screaming.
They called Anne a witch. They knew it

wasn't simply a matter of figuring tiny green levers.

Reality Organization

1.
4:30 a.m. with the woe adding up
in notches on your gut-wall,
guilts, indignities, whatever, there's no sleep,
you're bright, you "keep up," you know what's what, but
this isn't the time when you want to know everything's nothing

but some few subatomic elements skeetering
through emptiness, what seem the solid edges of things
are hazinesses of particle give-and-take and "really"
must look like continual maelstrom, and people you love
are whole new sets of cells each 7 years—no,

that's all fine to know but now you simply want
to walk with some dignity to the shed, and
press your forehead to the russian olive there, its trunk
unyielding, a thing not you but able to texture you,
a hardness to hold to, a firm true specific event.

2.
Zen and the Art of Computer Management Systems.
Holistic Bioengineering: A Home Cassette Series.
Alternate Consciousness and Corporation Profile—A Symposium.
By now it's no secret: scientific method,
the Newtonian/Cartesian paradigm, isn't hauling ass

and soul in happy tandem very well. And so
(as one book says) "to use an obvious example," war
we calibrate down to the leastmost ladybug's-waist-sized
chainmail link and up to megaton trajectory, we
artfully assemble, Trojan H and H-bomb, but

what makes us make war, what demanding psyche-ghosts
howl down the spiral staircase
of our genes—"we are no closer to this
understanding now than, say, in Hellenistic times." They
had *Lysistrata*. We have biofeedback and we have *Lysistrata*.

3.
We have biofeedback. We know there are levels
where light's too large to land, so "being" anything isn't
being visible or countable—levels where dream is
logic, levels where you could fall lost in the space
between your own hand and its shadow. Maybe a God,

even a God of terrible vengeance, is less frightening
than floating through physics. The God says:
Here are boundaries; this and this are real, this not.
The God says: Things actually do add up. We love
to add. The name of Allah was *26,000*

times stitched into a 16th century Turkish warship's pennant.
There are an estimated *4 million* mummified ibises
in an Egyptian labyrinth offered unto Thoth.
We love to tally. The rosary's abacus beads.
The first worked stones are scored.

4.
It was nearly dawn when I found you. By then
you were calm. That tree had punished you or healed you
or simply been a symbol of something reliably
beyond the tormenting refinements of human confusion.
Your skin was moire from the bark—your sadness,

leached out by that contact. I led you back
into the house. Or you could have been leading me—that's
not the point. I know we can't approach the universe

as if its secrets are quantifiable, not any more. And even
so, I know we all deserve the reassurance

of weight and number, perimeter, durability. Some
days both of those opposing knowings pull, and early
sun in a slant through the basketball net
mandalas the shed—my eyes can spin in there,
electronwise, wholegalaxyclusterwise, and not be wiser.

Some Things

I'm tired of writing about the gods,
those causal winds we snap in.
Tired of reading their signs in the entrails
when the guts themselves, the fat swags
of an animal, are eloquent enough.
And: if-the-universe-is-expanding-what-
is-it-expanding-*into* . . .   I'm tired

of all of it, I'm weary of every gasleak
of abstraction. Conscience. Self-determination.
Omniscience. Lassitude. Free will.
The ancient rabbis fasted, prayed
and fasted, finally they were Spirit,
flew through air, *were* air, were air
on fire around His throne, and

still returned to an umber mug
of cabbage soup in the morning.
Checking the goat in the pen; she
birthed the night before, her vulva
one engorged carnation
with paprika-spots of blood. I may
require theophany after too many

things, but for now give me things.
For now, they have the power of liturgy
off a cuneiform tablet—absolute and hard.
The 6th-grade class once left "a thank you note
for Nick at Twin Donut." It goes like this:
*We saw the deep fryer, the oil, the kitchen,
the rising place for the dough.*

As Response

This friend believes in God; and the light
falls, milled by the living whirr of the boughs,
to our feet, in a pile of dazzling rags.
This other friend doesn't; and still,
all afternoon, one way or another, the light
descends with the dust of the stars
and the dander of rats' backs,
in its ever-arriving body, to our bodies,
and *now* what, and why do they look to me
for a resolution? I can only say, and this
is as response but not as answer, that
the verdigrised patina and hairnet cracks
of junk in cluttered emporia dedicated to junk
have always called me: chipped kitsch
Jesuses revealing their hearts like an act
through a circus tent-flap and, alongside,
globby-eyed ceramic hula cuties frozen in a sway
of their peeking nicked hips; old toys,
the windup springs of which unspooled like metal tickertape
decades ago, and still this organ grinder's monkey
stuck in mid-cavort, this pair of one-time
circles-spinning celluloid waltzers, say
our pleasures, if we're lucky, really do find simple and
clarified form; glass "diamonds"; gum trading cards;
1950s "boomerang" and "amoeba" ashtrays; aromatic
piles of pamphlets, advising on structuring
tuna loaf, on mixing the long-outmoded drinks of 1943
in long-outmoded hiball shaker sets with jitterbugging
pink elephants rounding their sides, on how
the love of the Lord will see you through something
repeatedly called "Adversity," on how the supersalesman

"on the go-go-GO" will "not just step but PEP" his
foot successfully wedged in a customer's door—and all this
paper, stained, discarded, testimony to years lived
fully humanly, wearing its boas of mould . . .   One
time I attended a flea market with somebody, she
strode out in ten minutes: bored, I believe, and a little
repulsed. All of her own possessions were new.
The grander idea of history and the lesser idea
of fingerprints, she didn't want them
commemorative in her day. And so we walked the lakeside.
Yes, but what does she think? just tell me that: the oxygen we
rerumple into our chests all night is untouched
by the dead? the chosen units of the world we hug to desperately
are something other than recombination? we
don't step every morning out into the field
of beautiful brutal used light?

Domains

July. The ragweed's ultramealy sex is in the air
and, with the window wide for breeze, is in whatever
damp reception-pits my cranium throws
open to such drift. The tradeoff's halfass cool
for fullblown clog, and nothing's going to please me.
8 p.m. I close the window when the viciousness of 12-year-olds
across the street accrues too much: "You fartface,
Julie! You asshole ass!"—from one. And from another:
"Drooley Julie eats booooogers! Go rot with boogers!"
She does go—crying, I can see, and from what I can see
her major crime is she's twice the size of the others, tush
a gravity-sagging target just begging for insult, and
a set of Asian/Negro features mixed past the borders of peer
acceptability. A truly shitty day. Although

I lug up *Peritoneum to Quagga* to bed: *Pollen*
is, it turns out (as by irony
our nemeses often are), beautiful: some spin about like planets
of cathedrals, with their complex Gothic architecture
spired pole to pole; corsages, panpipes, freeway systems
of pollen, starbursts of pollen, honeyglazed hams. And
"the underwater flowering plant" of the Mediterranean
Sea, Posidonia, waves in fields of flat-green
ribbon-like leaves: "the stamens discharge their pollen
as long threads floating away in search of fertilization."
—Milt-pollen! Undulant otherworld meadows
of otherblossoms, where "air" is ocean; "breezes," ocean currents;
"drowning," living . . .   What a wondrous thing to dim with
into dream . . .   Where Otherme

---

cowers or struts in his Also-gestalt, at home
in the logics, at home in the lusts, of Otherhome . . .   When
Skyler finally eases into bed, and angles and re-angles
comfy composition of self and sheet, then puffs her
sleepbreath down my neck, an alien presence, an intimate fit,
the nudging bump of rump on rump in darkness . . .   I'm
awake in any case, sinuses full-tilt into sludge production.
I trudge downstairs, defeated by my own tissues and even
so, amazed at how lucky we are we love each other this
way this much. Sitting by that window: I'm in moonlight's living
silverplating. Well, actually I'm triangulating sunlight.
There are so many domains. And Julie doesn't know it
yet, but she's traveling through time at ferocious rate. She's
going to live in another world. She's going to be someone's flower.

Toil,

rhymes with *soil.* The craftsman Snedjem
and his wife are—in the painting at Deir el-Medina—working
the land. A lower register shows them
plowing (toil also half-rhymes *till*) with the typical
horn-yoked spotted heifers of Egyptian mural art.
And in an upper band the scythe he holds he holds
two-handed; filament-like stalks in its curve are caught so
fine and straight, the look is of Snedjem learning
the harp. And it's true: while this is labor ankle-caked
in earth, it isn't Earth. Its lineation may be loyal

to Earth in a vague way, but this is a tomb painting, and
these Snedjem figures labor in the afterlife, the "Fields of Yalu"
—eternal corn, and its eternal requirements. "May I be able
in the tomb to eat, drink, plough, and reap"—the *Book of the
        Dead.* So
toil is our conduit; and even without a credible Heaven, the buried
work their dirt. Tell *that* to Degas' laundress,
all the air gone blearily *sfumato* with the feel
of her own late-hour weariness leaking steamily out
while she presses, and night presses her. Or tell it,
go ahead, to the drill-switch assistant on top of the oil

derrick a WPA Arts-in-Communities Project has placed
on a 1930s post office wall. This far from shore
this high, the gulls and clouds confuse where Earth dominion
ends. Sweat slicks his back, so does the salt air always
rubbing up against him like a tease—and so the line between
the work and the world, the task and its context,
blurs. In fact, he likes his job; he enters aerial
risk like a gym towel into its snap—one-two,

lean and pizzazzy. And even so, I wouldn't tell him
how endless it's going to be, I wouldn't spoil

the moment by saying it could be any moment forever.
The best of our looks at forever suggest it, though. "Angel"
means "messenger"; so they have their jobs, it isn't all
one choral hallelujah loafing on cumulonimbus. They deliver—they
    bear the
impossible idea, the fiery sword,
annunciations leave their lips in scroll-like pennants
and they'll wrestle us if necessary, not easily
either but nightlong, groaning, even when they win
they fly off weakened by the contact. Maybe some of them
do plow, for all we know. In an oil

painting by Jan Van Eyck from 1432, an angel
plays the organ. Note how we say "playing"; but
a similar scene in a French book 10 years earlier shows
the back side of a similar organ, with—as had to be,
then—one more angel, kneeling, working (note
how we say "working") the hand-bellows that
enables the keys to "make" music. Praise is their major labor.
Why do we die? a joke soberly goes. *Because we're the angels'
abbreviation.* Then: *our* labor is *their* praise-making
condensed to the limited human vessel, until it reaches boil,

pains us maybe, describes an intensity certainly, then
escapes and goes wherever anything acorporeal finally
goes . . .   We must remember this. It's
praise, of a kind, he's building unit by unit up there.
His hair smells like the derrick by now, his spit does.
Wind wants his body. Oh but he's saving it for
this laundress he knows, he's going to give what's left
by the end of a rig shift to that sweet pink
sugarslit inside her thatch. They're going to jelly her roll,
then going to rest. Now he rivets. He watches the ocean roil.

The Gate

Often I miss the old poems, the High Ones:
the sober Miltonian cosmosgestalt-explainers,
with the lobes of gods like batteries
charging the lightningfork and discourse of their iambics;
or the stately, convolute Modernist epics
taking us by either anthro- and psycho- logical hand
through the filedrawered corridors of our learning;
or, of course, the anonymous
ritual incantations of the priestesses
as the cord was cut, or the crops beseeched
or the New Year ushered in on the oil-anointed back of a
    honey-fed bull,
parnassian, empyrean, hierophantic
—*those* poems. Now, it's more
the way I've seen you float in sun in sleep, like the meat
of the tangerine in its richly sugared marmalade holding; more
the singular snailtrack of slobber
down the retarded boy's pink jaw; the fading jetstreak
of a lie from out of another cloned politico's mouth,
zip, gone, but here forever; how
I'll stand below the block's lone oak
in darkness, sometimes, almost as if the wind is
tumbling leaves up there like tickets in some universe-wide lottery
and I'm straining to glimpse the numbers of those I love . . .   it's
dark, I *can't* see, but I listen there long minutes . . .
Last night I had to leave the party
for a moment, walk without even being sure why
from the loose, boozey circles of conversation and tympani ice-clink,
to the silence of our hosts' tree-posted back yard.
What impelled me . . .   I knew so much of the lives
inside, their small betrayals and charities,

all the cabriole-twists in their otherwise straightshaped reaching
toward a perfectly bedrock happiness . . . So many had settled
for less. Some composition of the room had made the air a prism
these lives converged in, shooting out an invisible ray
that burned its way into my chest. Outside,
the night air cooled this wound a little. The stars
kept me from flying away, like sprinkled salt in that folk story
grounding a bird. I was okay, then. I could think calmly
of what had gone wrong with us,
why, and its possible righting; think, without a hurt
    that overpowered,
of the words you'd used like scalpels on the part of my life
I'd made naked to you; and think,
without too much confusingly hopeful application, of how
emptiness is an alias of potential, what
that means for the space that's awake between us
when we sleep. Then I could walk back
in; the party was still at peak. We blathered
Joan's affair with Ramon, and what the state legislature would do
instead of raise taxes, there was dill-&-onion dip and a thumblength
too much gin for the tonic, something about the new laser
technology for rock discs, something cinema, something
everything and nothing, then you looked at me and said
as everybody was saying one way or another about how
it was time to leave, and yes it was time, and so we left,
back to our days, one could say to our fate, between
where the Angels with the sword and the palm-frond
guarded each side of the Gate.

One Continuous Substance

A small boy and a slant of morning light
both exit the last dark trees of this forest, though
the boy is gone in an instant. Not

the light: it travels its famous 186,000 miles per second
to be this still gold bar
on the floor of the darkness. I suppose

that from the universe's point of view
we do the same: a small boy and an old man
being one continuous substance.

We were making love when the phone rang
saying my father was dead, and the sun
kept touching you, there, and there, where I'd been.

How the World Works: An Essay

That's my topic. How complex, Alhambran arabesques of weather
(seen computer-screened by satellites); and the weathering eddies
    on tiles
in the courtyards and intimate tryst-rooms and policy chambers
of The Alhambra itself: construe a grander pattern.
How the west wind whipples the osiers. How the slivery, eyeless
cave fish in Mexico slip through their fissures unerring.
In Nepal, a poacher reams a spoonful of musk
from that orifice near the urethra, holding—with his other
gloved hand—the deer's small death-kicks steady; and in
mid-Manhattan at 3 a.m., at Chico's place, the Pimp Prince
enters swimming in coke, with one new frou-frou dewy-cunted
acolyte on each eelskin sleeve, and he reeks of a vial
of musk. I'm singing the rings-in-rings song of the planet,
its milks, its furnaces, its chlorophyll links. One

suddenly clear blue afternoon (when I was 8) of the kind
Lake Michigan unhoards at winter's thinner end,
the sky: a child soprano's pure high-C struck after
months of ugly gutturals . . . a copper (as my father still
referred to them), a copper of the old school, beefy, easy, from
the one-foot-on-the-runningboard days of Chicago ticketdom,
stopped us *slam* in the midst of our shoreline spree, the flasher
calling all of Heaven's attention, I thought, to this misfortunate
second-hand dent-bodied Chevy. "Officer, have you had
breakfast?" "Why, no sir." And he wetted his finger and thumb
(he always did this with money) and from (as my father
still called a wallet) his billfold, a 5 (you could do it for 5
in those days) sleeked on over. Later, educative and high on this
his mastery, he winked and told me that was how the world

worked. This was part of an interlocked system for him as
sure as the ecoconnectedness in the italic stance of a cattle egret,
the living shoulders it tweezes, lice that graze this egret's
feather-flesh, and dungbugs shitting the bull's more generous
shit back incremental and rich to the grasses . . . all
neat, clean, a perfect processional circle of textbook arrows.
So: you invited "the Boss" to dinner and used
the holiday silver and chortled at jokes which
were "a riot," and thus you "advanced"; you shmoozed
the waitress, and her service upgraded. This was a very clear
flow chart, and I sing the song of its unctious functioning-well.
I was 8: I believed him. He believed himself. For
thousands of years, for that matter, the planet revolved
Ptolemaically, managing beautifully, thank you. Once

a woman I knew in my days of believing repeated sex
meant knowing a person, said, from out of some vaporous cranial
nowhere, "Do you think we come from monkeys, or little
enemas in the water?" and after the ripplings of pity and comedy
through me, I began the task of explaining the planet: I still
have the cocktail napkin that cartoonily shows Earth
axis-spit and pivoting, and that crudely rules a B.C./A.D. timeline.
This was long ago; I'd like to apologize, now, for that
initial pity: once I saw the tiny beads of bravery she needed
to restring each morning just to face the next
dyslexic day, I understood—too late to do love any good—
the shadows she walked through the rest of us didn't. And
by then of course I'd also come to understand my father
wasn't sharp or slick but small in a way

that makes me tender toward him: one more anyone
with his salesman's satchel, and son, and wife, like counters
in some global game, "Advantage," tycoons and brigadiers play. Well
now he's *in* the globe, beyond maneuvering. I saw him
lowered; now he's part of the parfait striations I'm singing of,
part of the nitrogen / flywheel / hovel-and-palace totalityworks
called Terra—where the butterfly fish
at mating time, the vivid-hued and specifically-patterned
butterfly fish, fights rivals with its colors for weapons,
its cinnabars and its veridians, deepening, quivering, them . . .
while out back of Chico's, the Pimp Prince stands
his gaudy ground in front of a would-be usurper,
plumed hats, ostrich boots, gold neckchains,
one a ruby ring, one jade . . . Oh the world

not only works but networks, rarefiedly, in
topnotch geewhillikers form. The ever-ravenous protozoa
in the rumen-goop of that bull I earlier mentioned, burbling
away at their cellulose walls . . . by one hashbrowns-surrounded
breakfast steak, they *are* connected to some soul-weary
salesman in 1929 pulling in to a roadside diner architected to be a
giant coffee pot on Pacific Highway outside South Tacoma.
Let the sign of that connection be the thready, heady
olfactory-waft of ant saliva the anteater rides like radar
unto its repast. And so there *is* a mode, an almost diagrammable
order, albeit on levels sub and supra while we sit around
in the dark with our luminous human desires confusing the
everything that they're a part of. Still we need
to remember, against our own small breakdown days. Once

after my father had died but before the family car was sold
I joyrode with a lady, one-handed wheeling us up
the curves past Lighthouse Point. A cop clocked our speed:
an hour later I was in custody—a shabby, crapped-up,
roach-infested custody—for attempting to bribe. It was
bad, but I was good, and it was brief. What's longer and
sticks with me more is being dropped off back at the car,
too tired even to feel defeated, somewhere on damp sand
miles from anywhere 3 or 4 in the morning. When
the engine wouldn't turn, that last indignity, all I could do
was sit stupidly humming—not singing just humming—
on the hood, and stare at the first gray rhythmic swashing
in-and-out of the water, sure that nothing ever does, or
ever had really, or ever would, work.

The Sciences Sing a Lullabye

Physics says: go to sleep. Of course
you're tired. Every atom in you
has been dancing the shimmy in silver shoes
nonstop from mitosis to now.
Quit tapping your feet. They'll dance
inside themselves without you. Go to sleep.

Geology says: it will be alright. Slow inch
by inch America is giving itself
to the ocean. Go to sleep. Let darkness
lap at your sides. Give darkness an inch.
You aren't alone. All of the continents used to be
one body. You aren't alone. Go to sleep.

Astronomy says: the sun will rise tomorrow,
Zoology says: on rainbow-fish and lithe gazelle,
Psychology says: but first it has to be night, so
Biology says: the body-clocks are stopped all over town
and
History says: here are the blankets, layer on layer, down and down.

Albert Goldbarth is Distinguished Professor of Humanities at Wichita State University and the author of numerous collections of prize-winning poetry, including *Popular Culture* and *Arts & Sciences*. He is also the author of a recently published collection of essays, *A Sympathy of Souls*.

The Contemporary Poetry Series

EDITED BY PAUL ZIMMER

The Contemporary Poetry Series

EDITED BY BIN RAMKE